Sales Demystified

An Insider's Guide to Building Better Sales Professionals

Steve Rangoussis

HOCKEYSTICK GROWTH PUBLISHING

D.B.A. Feature Reality
PO Box 751270
Petaluma, California 94975

Copyright © 2020 by Steve Rangoussis

ISBN: 978-1-7350092-0-9

Edited by Greg Brown

Interior Design by Christina Suh

Cover Design by Daniel Ojedokun

For Eliana, Jason, Kalista and Leonidas

My greatest accomplishment in life.

TABLE OF CONTENTS

Introduction

Salespeople and some non-salespeople alike understand there are salespeople and then there are . . . well . . . salespeople. The same holds true for sales leaders, most of whom were successful individual contributor sales representatives (reps) at some point. For simplification let's just bundle both leaders and reps into the "sales professionals" bucket.

Many sales professionals love what they do. Others live in a perpetual state of misery. With the right leadership, miserable sales professionals can thrive and be happy with match quality, skill development, and direction, while those above-average performers who already love what they do can become significantly better through good coaching[i]. That's partly why this book exists: to provide insight on sales professionals' development. However, this book is just as important for coworkers in non-sales functions, such as software engineers, finance, or company founders, serving to demystify what happens in the sales realm.

This book is comprised of two parts: the first is focused on front line sales reps; the second looks at sales leaders. Regardless of one's role, the book should be read in its entirety to gain a holistic perspective and reap the greatest benefit. It's important to note I'm intentionally using a conversational style. While some may be slightly put off by my candor and perhaps my humor, if I were in front of you, this is likely how I would speak with you and the approach I would take. So,

I'm being honest, and earnest, two things, as we'll learn later, that are crucial in both life and sales. Humans are hardwired to remember stories, so I've sprinkled in truly personal anecdotes to underscore important lessons. The only things I've changed in the stories are the names, which I've altered in an attempt to protect the innocent (and the guilty). In the end, you will have actionable insights for understanding and improvement, all delivered through a conversational tone and via the insight and power of story. That's my hope for our time together at least.

This next part of the introduction is mainly for those who aren't sales professionals, though sales professionals should probably read this part for recognition.

Sales is the lifeblood of business. Sales = execution. The best idea, product, or service must be sold. If it can't be sold, it's dead on arrival, and the business will cease to exist, period! That favorite electronic component, that wearable you love, someone sold that in bulk near the front of the supply chain. Now you benefit from how aesthetically and functionally pleasing it is.

Externally, from the smallest component part in production, to the most elaborate piece of machinery, sales professionals are responsible for market realization.

Internally, selling across functions or selling up to management moves the business forward, agnostic of role or position. That means if you're an engineer, and especially if you have direct reports, you're in a "non-sales selling" role, as Daniel Pink puts it in *To Sell Is Human.* In his book, Pink proves through activity analysis that more than 40 percent of time is devoted to internal selling related activity. Sales is all around us, and when done right, it leads to positive outcomes.

But there's a stigma about sales professionals. That they are over-bearing, aggressive, and manipulative individuals who strong-arm clients into acquiescing to purchase. Perhaps some of that was the case a long time ago. Those who don't know have unfortunately adopted those infamous traditional characteristics even though they're the antithesis of what works in today's buying environment. True sales professionals are actually extremely helpful, knowledgeable, and adept at addressing customer needs. True sales professionals do not come off as though they are selling at all. They are seamless.

What qualifies me to be an expert on the subject?

This is where I'm supposed to outline a sales pedigree going back to my great-great-great grandpappy, who was the first sales pioneer in our family. If I did that, I'd be lying. The truth is I got into sales you can say by accident. I helped a stranger and his wife out years ago. They were appreciative, and the stranger offered me a sales job at his company, a rep agency.

If I hadn't been deep in the hole with debt after college and unemployed with no viable job prospects on the horizon, I probably would have passed on the opportunity. I'd probably be writing a cookbook right now. Later, I discovered the rep agency was under pressure from the main manufacturer they represented to hire someone to replace a rep who should have retired about a decade sooner. They were just as desperate as me!

For my first foray into sales, I was a full commission independent sales rep. That means the agency secured product lines, and I sold those products in a clearly defined territory for a commission—a split commission, actually, where the agency principals took 45 percent of my commission earnings while I retained 55 percent. The commission average for the manufacturers we represented was about 5 percent. So, if I sold $1,000 worth of product, I earned $27.50 before taxes. Yay! Of course, I had to pay for all my own expenses, including travel, vehicle, meals, electronics, and the like. On top of all that glory, I had to pay double the social security tax, plus file as an independent contractor with the IRS.

Being a full commission rep, or a *fool* commission rep, depending on how you look at it, meant living a feast or famine lifestyle. I was already in debt. Though I had no sales training, I had things to sell and a small-but-existing customer base with established product lines. I had no choice really but to figure out how to be successful mostly on my own. I jumped in with both feet. I showed up to my first day on the job armed with the product catalogs I'd been studying and dressed in my best (and only) suit.

The agency principals, Bob and Tom (not their real names), met me at their office, where I learned my first sales lesson. After going through assigned territory accounts, Bob, a combination elder statesman and hustler, along with his partner, Tom, a middle-aged, former AAA baseball player, cut to the chase.

"You have your territory, your product lines. How are you going to be successful and make us proud?" Bob asked.

"I'm going to study these catalogs and memorize all the product features to start," I said naively.

"Steve, don't do that to yourself!" Bob exclaimed. "There are thousands of products in there for hundreds of different kinds of customers."

"Yeah," Tom added, "we've been doing this for over twenty years, and we don't know a third of that stuff."

"Well then I'm open to suggestions," I said perplexed.

Tom pushed into my personal space, raised his chest against mine, and used his index finger to convey his point. "Don't bullshit anyone! If you don't know something, say you'll find out, because the second you do bullshit someone, you'll lose all trust. Besides, you can't bullshit a bullshitter!"

We all laughed, one of us uncomfortably. I turned to walk out of the office toward my car, ready to embark on my sales journey, when Bob launched a final salvo.

"One more thing," he said. "Don't ever come in here or go into any of your accounts dressed like that. You'll make everyone nervous looking like a goddamn lawyer!"

Looking back, those formative, and often uncomfortable, sales years are best described as a classic baptism by fire. I learned the hard way what worked and what didn't, including what advice to follow from Bob and Tom. "No BS" is cardinal rule number one in sales (pay attention folks whose mantra is "fake it till you make it"). Product knowledge and knowing which application is best suited for which purpose are of paramount importance, too, regardless of Bob and Tom's take. I also took every opportunity to learn directly from the manufacturers we represented, either through product trainings they offered, or when riding with sales managers and product managers when they visited my territory.

By year five at the agency, I was a top-performing sales rep, out of debt, and had some meager savings. I must have made an impression because accounts gave my name to a multinational company with a subsidiary in my territory that was looking for a regional sales rep to cover eleven states as one of their first sales hires. They offered premium products, a base salary plus performance bonus, benefits, a company car, and an expense account that was seemingly bottomless the first few years.

Within the first year of becoming a regional sales rep, I had outperformed everyone at that company by a significant margin. We were growing like crazy. We started hiring more sales reps, and I was training them on sales fundamentals and territory management. Eventually, I was promoted to Sales Director West. As we kept crushing goals and growing exponentially, I became the first VP of

Sales. After eleven years at the company, I was promoted to Chief Sales Officer for the North America HQ.

We had grown more than seventeen times into a midsized company and become the top subsidiary. We bought an additional thirty acres of land where we were planning on building a production facility in front of our United States HQ, doubling the size of our office and warehouse. We had the full support of the mothership back in Europe. Additionally, we helped change an industry from one that was conditioned to buy cheap products, to one that was willing to pay a premium for innovative products that had greater benefits with longer lifespans.

Working for this multinational company was the highlight of my career, not just because of the success we achieved together, but also because I formally and informally learned sales and leadership techniques that work. The company spared no expense in developing its people including me. I learned different sales methodologies, studied sales leadership at major universities, earned sales management certificates to further augment my expertise, went back to school for an MBA to become more well-rounded in business, and learned in the field from some of the most progressive sales leaders at the time. I was able to experiment and implement new sales initiatives; design territories, create sales training curriculums for new and existing staff; and roll-out creative, team-building strategies among other things.

I must have missed the chaos, uncertainty, and struggle I experienced early on in my sales career, though, because I gave it all up to break into Silicon Valley tech as a sales leader. My position was comfortable, my future was predictable, and my influence in the industry was respectable. And then I walked away from what some might call the perfect job.

I was fortunate. I eventually secured a VP of Sales position for a series A funded technology startup, supported by a who's-who list of investors. Intellectually, the company was at the next level. Most of the staff were graduates from top-tier schools and had advanced degrees. I built out its sales organization. Along the way, I learned the intricacies of working at technology startups. That fast-paced, intense, and ever-changing environment was a shot in the arm that forced me to grow further as a sales professional.

Since parting ways with that tech company, I've been offering advice as a sales leadership consultant for local businesses as well as for Silicon Valley venture capital portfolio companies where my background can benefit more people and those who need it most. There are some amazing people doing incredible things that are impacting the world. These people have great ideas. They have created innovative products or services. They just need help selling from sales organizational infrastructure to deal close. That's where I come in.

I've seen a lot, lived through a ton, studied successful sales organizations, read volumes of sales-related books, experimented with sales methodologies, and so on. I'm still learning new things, usually around technology, but the sales fundamentals remain constant. My purpose is to impart some of that knowledge on to you. After being in sales deliberately for nearly twenty-five years across industries and in different positions, I hope I've earned your trust. And, in case you were wondering, I still live and breathe cardinal rule number one: I won't bullshit you!

CHAPTER 1

The Ten Commandments of Sales Success

L et's start our journey together here with a brief rundown of what I call the ten commandants of sales success. After establishing the takeaways, we'll dive more deeply into each commandment, solidifying your foundation into successful selling. While you won't find the kind of glib, ribbing advice that Bob and Tom dumped on me all those years ago, I'm hopeful you will find actionable tasks, a shift in your sales mindset, and enough inspiration to start realizing your own career ambitions.

1. Thou shalt not bullshit.

To earn a customer's trust, the salesperson must be sincere. Successful sales professionals admit when they don't have the answers and are willing to potentially lose a sale to gain a long-term customer. They keep their word and fall on their sword when they are wrong.

2. Thou shall be intentional.

Achievement orientation is a major driver for successful sales professionals. Their laser focus on goals shields them from distractions and allows them to keep getting maximum results from concerted efforts. Elite sales professionals are prepared and organized. They dedicate the necessary time in advance of meetings to ensure they're ready to do their best. They are mindful of the limited time of the customer and aim to provide something of value with every meeting.

3. Thou shall have a high sense of urgency.

World class sales professionals, "Leave nothing for tomorrow which can be done today," as Abraham Lincoln once said. They respond immediately to customers, move quickly (and methodically) to get proposals in as soon as possible, and keep their pipeline flowing at all times. They know that opportunity waits for no one.

4. Thou shall have a winning attitude.

Own everything and stay positive. Top sales professionals control their own destiny by having the mindset that they are responsible for what happens to them. They have a positive mental attitude, see the positive in every situation, and remain optimistic particularly around customers.

5. Thou shall be resourceful.

Elite sales professionals find creative ways to solve problems. They know how to leverage the expertise of others and explore alternatives to keep the customer happy. They identify ways to address the needs of the customer and go the extra mile to satisfy those needs.

6. Thou shall have grit.

Rejection, obstacles, and stalled deals are par for the course. Gritty sales professionals celebrate and focus on their victories, regardless of whether they are minor or major. They simply don't dwell on what the uninitiated would consider failure, because there is no failure—only steps in the process and adjustments to be made in order to move sales forward.

7. Thou shall be communicative.

The ability to listen intently is found among sales professional elites. These individuals are respectful of the customer's time and speak carefully to address the customer's needs. They listen twice as much as they speak, even with their most dedicated customers.

8. Thou shall be enthusiastic.

The best sales professionals recognize that enthusiasm is contagious. Expressing belief in a product or service with conviction can make the difference between getting the sale and losing the sale. If the person selling isn't enthusiastic about what they're offering, why should the customer be?

9. Thou shall be an expert.

Top sales professionals are knowledgeable about their offerings. They know details that are too nuanced to find independently. They use their experience and understanding to position themselves to best give product or service advice.

They are prepared with a working knowledge of the customer's application, the problem that needs to be solved, and are ready to discuss how their offering is best suited to be the solution.

10. Thou shall be empathetic.

Successful salespeople empathize with customers. Having empathy allows the sales professional to take on the customer's perspective which then informs the best solution to the customer's problem. Empathy also plays a humanitarian role because it encourages the salesperson to have integrity and sell what is necessary for the customer while remaining honest about nice to haves. To be clear, empathy does not mean discounting products in order to be nice, it means putting oneself in the customer's shoes and be treated the way you would expect to be treated.

A Deep Dive into the Ten Sales Commandments

I managed to apply that *first sales commandment* shortly after I was out in my territory on my own when I met up with a top account. My predecessor purposely stayed away from meetings with this account because he'd been warned they had a tendency to pepper their reps with highly technical questions. I came prepared with the latest promotions and updated collateral for the account.

The owner, Jack, was a dark-haired, middle age man who spoke like an English lit professor and carried himself like a corporate executive. He intercepted me at the front of the office before I could go any further. I introduced myself, and he immediately asked me about my background.

I explained that I wasn't from the industry. I wasn't even an end user of the products. But I was learning fast and had inside knowledge on how best to advise him on how to help grow his business by buying smart with our offerings. I also assured him I was a fast learner and genuinely interested in getting up to speed on the products.

"Well, it's a start," he said, signaling me to follow him as he gave me the nickel and dime tour of the facility.

After putting my best foot forward while informing him of the upcoming promotions, and changing out the collateral, which was several years old, I thanked him for his time. As he quietly followed me out, he said, "By showing up here you're already better than our previous rep. By being honest when you walked in, you are better than the rest of my reps."

Later I came to find out that Jack was a tenured rep himself. He'd sold premium products as a sales rep like me, until he made the leap to become a distributor and sell products to discriminating customers who only wanted the best. I ended up having a great relationship with Jack for many years, and we remain in touch today. Our relationship, like the best relationships, has been reciprocal. While I assisted him in growing his business with my products, he served in some ways as a mentor and an active reference later in my career. If I had fallen back on bullshit, as human nature sometimes seems to urge us to do in challenging times where we're unsure or insecure, I would have missed the chance for a lifelong connection.

*

As a full commission sales rep, I had to be intentional and in so doing, live the *second sales commandment* in order to survive.

When I left my home in the morning, I knew exactly how much I had to sell to cover my expenses. I knew where I was tracking for the month, and where I needed to be for the quarter. At the end of the day,

I would go through invoices that landed and write the amounts on a whiteboard calendar in my bedroom, where it was the first thing I saw in the morning.

Before Google Maps, I had to methodically plan out my route and set up account appointments to be as efficient as possible without sacrificing time, all while allowing for buffers so appointments wouldn't bleed into each other. There was very little room for mistakes, which were costly, so I had to be intentional about everything I did.

*

Energy and urgency get noticed. The *third sales commandment*, a high sense of urgency, is a great way to stand out. These days it seems fewer sales reps have a high sense of urgency. I've personally found technology makes it easier to reply to customers faster. It also makes it easier to set triggers reminding you to follow through on your follow ups. When I was a rep, I checked my messages and email frequently, responding right away, even if it was just to let a customer or colleague know I received their message but needed more time to investigate before delivering a complete answer. As a result, people started seeing me as reliable and dependable. Not only that, people tended to treat my requests with the high sense of urgency I treated theirs.

Nowadays, we are bombarded with information and relentlessly pinged with email notifications and social media updates. Perhaps this helps explain the distractions sales professionals now face, but it doesn't get to the missing motivation or lack of urgency that I see among so many sellers now. Your customer (and your boss) come *first*. Before your friend's latest escapade that was just posted on social media. If you get a message as a rep, you *must* reply as soon as you're available.

Time delays kills sales. Buyers get cold feet. The competition sweeps in to secure the order before you had a chance to send over your proposal as you waited on someone internally who was dragging their feet. My team lost significant amounts of sales, and even lost a large account after courting it for over a year, under just such a circumstance. It was a large opening order, and alongside my signature, we also needed the CFO's signature on the final contract. I explained to the CFO the importance of getting this deal to the finish line as soon as possible. I reminded him in person, over email, text, and phone. The response? Crickets. After well over a month passed, the deal got cold. Anger stands the hairs on the back of my neck straight up when I think of it now as it's completely unacceptable for there to be a lack of urgency involving sales.

Recently I've come across salespeople who take days just to acknowledge receipt of a message. Beyond that, there isn't even a follow up. Some claim they only communicate through text and didn't reply to emails for a week. Almost all claim they were too busy, which is like slapping you in the face. As if you're not busy, too, and your time isn't valuable as well.

Whatever the excuse, if you're a sales professional without a high sense of urgency, there are other professions you're better suited for. Do yourself, your coworkers, and your prospective customers a favor and change careers.

*

The *fourth sales commandment*, having a winning attitude, is absolutely essential! A winning attitude reinforces the belief that you control your own destiny and are ultimately responsible for your results, regardless of external influence. It also means competing against yourself to constantly improve and do better. Here are some tips and tricks I've learned over the years on keeping a winning attitude alive during the toughest times:

- Gratitude should be the foundation of your attitude. Take time every day to think about the little things in your life that would be difficult to do without. There are many people who will never have what you have. Keeping these things in mind and recognizing people and opportunities that benefit your situation as they arise will further bolster your gratitude. It's scientifically proven that gratitude makes for a healthier life both mentally and physically[ii].

- Keep your emotions in check, develop your emotional intelligence. In the heat of a volatile situation, a technique that has helped me is tactical breathing. Breath in slowly for three seconds. Hold three seconds. Breath out for three seconds. Then repeat the whole process for five sets. Combine that with seeing the forest through the trees by acknowledging that the present is just a step toward your ultimate long-term goal and has little bearing in the grand scheme of things.

- Make no excuses. When you get good at making excuses, it's hard to excel at anything else. Take control by influencing how something impacts your mood. What has happened to you is less important than how you handle it.

*

Being resourceful within corporate guidelines is the *fifth sales commandment*. To be clear, lone wolfs and loose cannons are frowned upon, so staying within the corporate parameters, ethics, and company mission is critical. Sales reps, especially those in the field, have some autonomy to be creative in overcoming obstacles. It's a skill that needs to be developed, though. If a sales rep ends up in a sales leadership role, tapping into one's resourcefulness becomes a common occurrence.

Take this instance for example. Once, our company had a next generation container shipped to us that rendered a lot of our existing stock obsolete. While we had a phased rollout plan to transition our distributors, systematically replacing the old product with the new, internally we were stuck with a large quantity of the old-style containers. Coming out of a particularly rough recession, we'd set aside a budget to do something special for our distributors during the December holiday season. I proposed an idea tackling both issues.

We'd take one of our flagship products, create a chocolate mold from a local chocolatier in its shape, and ship it in the obsolete containers as a thank you to our distributors with their final orders for the year. The reps would follow up when the products landed at the distributor in their territory. Not only did this greatly reduce the obsolete inventory, we gained a tremendous amount of good will from our distributors. The beauty: it cost us less than discarding the obsolete containers outright.

*

Grit not only serves as the *sixth sales commandment*, it is a characteristic found among successful professionals from company founders to the world's top professionals in their respective fields. Author and psychologist at the University of Pennsylvania, Angela Duckworth, conducted studies, including elite military training graduates and top corporate salespeople, to find out who was successful and why. The results of these studies are described in her book, *GRIT*, where she proves that while it's generally accepted by society that talent is what drives success, effort is twice as important in determining success[iii].

Sales reps may hear ten or more no's before they collect a yes. Dwelling on the yes's and accepting the no's as part of the process is one way to cope with the constant rejection. I had a sales rep on my team who used the no's as a way to build up the intensity of when he would get a solid yes, such as bringing on a new account. He equated the feeling as being similar to the quickening experienced in "The Highlander" movies, where the victor is jolted for an extended period of time as all the power and knowledge of a lifetime from his defeated immortal foe is transferred intensely into him. The rep's twist was the harder fought the victory, the greater the intensity he felt in the end.

There was a multi-location account I was courting for some time without making much progress. After nearly two years of resourcefully going from purchasing agent down to sales manager and staff at each location to get buy-in, I was finally granted a chance to speak with the company founder. He was a megalomaniac who drove a yellow Lamborghini. He was a shrewd businessman, and reluctant to even attempt to bring in a spattering of our products to try, products that were two to ten times the price of others found in the same category.

I came prepared, with grit and a refusal to be turned away. I knew there was a major tradeshow fast approaching. I proposed that I work the three-day show on his company's behalf. If he felt the show wasn't a success with my product line, he could keep all the profit, and I would never bother him again. He was speechless for a good minute, contemplating how to respond. Then he broke the silence with a wry smile and said, "In exchange for a portion of my booth, you'll sell stock without a purchase order, and regardless if I move forward, I keep all the sales without any inventory overhead costs?" I confirmed, and we had a deal.

To stack the cards in my favor, I invited existing customers who were in the database, advertised on our company website, and made sure inside sales would mention the show to any end customers calling who were within proximity of the show location. The result was that the show was a huge success for me but fairly slow for the other brands they (and other exhibitors) were trying to sell. My portion of the booth was constantly bombarded with customers, which attracted curious attendees (*behavioral contagion*) who had never heard of the products. With proof, I was able to highlight how my product line was a source of competitive advantage because nobody in the area carried it, and with the product line came a high-end clientele who would buy other products from him that were profitable. From that point on, I had his buy-in. All his stores carried the full line. He sent all his salespeople to our training center. And he became one of our top distributors at the time.

*

To be communicative means to make the customer the center of attention with effective communication. This is the heart of the *seventh sales commandment.*

Asking open-ended questions and looking for cues on when to interject product insights are good tactics to keep reps communicative. The rep needs to earn the right to speak, and the customer needs to feel comfortable first before accepting that right.

I remember a typical ride along with a sales rep who was struggling in his territory. After our second appointment, it was becoming painfully clear that the rep was dominating the conversation, not picking up on cues, and interrupting the customer. This had to change if he was to remain employed.

Before the last meeting of the day, we did a postmortem of the previous two account visits over some coffee. I pointed out the things he did well, such as his brand ambassadorship, product knowledge, and how he knew everyone by first name. Then I zeroed in on two things I wanted him to work on: listening intently and talking only one quarter of the time.

He disputed that he dominated the conversation at the previous appointments, until I showed him my notes from the last appointment we made. I'd jotted down the time ranges when he would speak. It came out to more than 80 percent. He didn't have a leg to stand on. To sweeten the pot, I said that if he listened intently at our last appointment and spoke less than a quarter of the time, we would go to a nice steak house for dinner. Otherwise it was a fast food franchise with gold arches.

Guess what happened? The rep listened so intently and was so careful to only say the most important things, that he spoke less than 20 percent of the time and picked up on important information he normally missed. He also landed a nice order and gained a new product commitment from the customer. The rep was so thrilled that he offered to buy my steak dinner, to which I replied I was off of red meat anyway. The best thing he could do, I said, was continue to challenge himself at every meeting to do the same. In the months and years that followed, this rep became one of our top producing salespeople.

*

Can you think of a situation where a salesperson, a professor, or a doctor delivered a piece of information with enthusiasm? How did it make you feel? Was it easy to remember? What about when the same type of professional did it without enthusiasm? Is it hard to remember? How did that make you feel?

Enthusiasm is the *eighth sales commandment* and the trait that punctuates a successful sales professional's style. You can't expect customers to get excited about your offering if you aren't enthusiastic. I'm not talking about acting like an over-the-top performer, just injecting some spirit and conviction into your delivery.

I saw the power of enthusiasm once when riding with a sales rep who was so enthusiastic it was contagious.

We arranged an appointment with a distributor that had multiple locations but was reluctant to stock in a meaningful way a new product that happened to be the most expensive in our product line. It was clear that it was the best product in its class, but at a price four times greater than the competition, the owner was reluctant to take the financial risk.

We met the President, Mr. Yamaguchi, a reserved soft-spoken executive, sitting behind his desk that was covered with disheveled paperwork and vendor collateral. He couldn't be any more different from Tommy, his rep, a gregarious and high energy salesperson with the uncanny ability to disarm any personality within two minutes of conversation. Unlike other reps, Tommy knew Mr. Yamaguchi on a first name basis.

After collecting information by letting Mr. Yamaguchi express his concerns, Tommy started asking open-ended questions that led to why bringing in this new product in quantity made a lot of sense. As the rep asked more questions, his voice became more spirited and his smile larger. Mr. Yamaguchi, probably without realizing, mirrored the tone and smile when responding.

Then the rep asked, "So how many per location to start?" and they both laughed.

"One to show and one to go," said the owner.

Tommy leaned back in his seat and threw up his arms. "Come on! We have accounts with one location that are bringing in a pallet worth."

"Really?" The owner was curious now. "How many do you think I should bring in?"

"Two pallets per location—one to show and one to go!"

They laughed again, but then Tommy told Mr. Yamaguchi enthusiastically that he needed to show his customers how much he believed in the new product by keeping a stacked pallet on display. He pushed Mr. Yamaguchi over the fence by charging for the second pallet only when the first one had sold through, which would trigger another pallet order. It was the first time anyone had sold so many units of this product in one purchase. The recurring order was a great set up as well.

Now imagine the same situation with a rep who said the same things without enthusiasm or charisma. I'm fairly confident we would have been kicked out of the meeting.

*

Things are fluid in sales. There's a steady stream of upgrades, new products, new services, tweaks, pricing—I get it: nothing sits still for long! I also get how bad it looks when reps have to constantly read off of marketing collateral to answer customer questions. The trick around this is knowing the core offerings and the flag ship products and services inside out. So, employ the *ninth sales commandment* and know your stuff!

There was a dominant capital equipment player in a pocket of the Pacific Northwest. I'd been trying to land them as a client for the better part of a year knowing I had to bring them on if I were to set up my territory for long-term success. Their purchasing agent and head of sales operations, Ethan, an articulate gentleman from Sri Lanka, was very nice yet very reluctant to give our company a chance. Ultimately, he needed to be convinced that I would support his outside sales staff, and we would have a true partnership.

I set up some core products to demo and provided some coffee and donuts for the early morning meeting. The entire sales team trickled in. Before I knew it, I was being hit with multilayered rapid-fire questions that really tested my product knowledge.

They would describe how a customer had a very niche application and ask what if any product the customer should use and why it was a better solution. There were a few cases where I told them we couldn't help; there wasn't a product fit. In the situations where our products made sense, though, I hit it out of the park.

For about an hour, I nailed every inquiry, drawing upon the products I knew intimately because I'd put the time in to really *learn* them. It got to the point where I was quoting pricing and part numbers off the top of my head in addition to discussing features and benefits specific for the customers.

My audience seemed blown away. I saw some give Ethan a thumbs up. Other people shook my hand and offered praise for my insight. A couple of reps asked me to accompany them later that day to visit accounts together. Immediately after that meeting, I had a signed contract and opening order. If I hadn't been prepared as an expert, though, it could have gone sideways fast, and I would have squandered my chances of ever landing that account.

Bottom line: sales professionals must know their core products and services.

*

Empathy isn't a term most people equate with sales, which is truly unfortunate. After all, having empathy is the single biggest character-istic that sets modern day sales professionals apart from traditional salespeople who have stigmatized the profession. It's also the *tenth sales commandment.*

Having the ability to empathize with the customer is a skill that gives the sales professional a huge advantage. Those who have honed the skill can immediately address the customer's needs and offer solutions that resonate. The salesperson appeals to them, becoming, in a sense, their hero. That's the ideal, of course. In many cases, it's unbalanced, though, and empathy comes across as false or manufactured, a real kiss of death in sales. Consider the salesperson who gives discounts unnecessarily, killing profitability. Or the salesperson who uses insin-cere empathy as a superficial ploy to get the customer to let down their guard in order to be over sold to. That's not empathy. That's manipulation.

Remember Tommy who sold those pallets of new products to that multilocation account? He was making an end user sales call on behalf of one of his accounts. He ended up at the personal shop of a surgeon who was interested in our products as a hobby. After going through the entire catalog, Tommy ended up convincing the doctor to buy nearly every product we offered! That rep probably still holds the record for largest single hobbyist order, but it was a perverted use of empathy to get a large sale. Even for a professional, which our products were designed for, that broad range of products purchased was completely unnecessary, and much more so for a home hobbyist. The rep's behavior was really unethical and bad for our profession.

There were numerous times where I empathized with customers to offer what was needed to address their application. In fact, I would usually offer three options: the bare minimum order, the suggested order, and the larger nice-to-have order, leaving it to the customer to decide which to select. I took this approach with B2C as well as B2B customers. Seldom did I have someone take the bare minimum, and those who did usually came back to get the items left off the suggested order. Reps like me who used empathy correctly built trust with customers. Those customers then became repeat customers, primarily because we didn't lead them astray.

A Note on Work Ethic and Competition

Sales professionals who lead their fields have a strong work ethic. The many I have known do not work regular hours, especially those who work in the field. Rather they do what it takes to get the job done and to hit their goals, particularly if they are behind.

This is an important distinction not only among best-in-class salespeople, but also among other professions. Sales professionals rarely have great work/personal boundaries. I'm guilty of it myself. We're continuously checking messages and working nights and weekends, slipping away from friends and family to take care of business.

By nature of the job, top sales professionals are very, very competitive. I alluded to this in the winning attitude section. Competition against oneself is essential in constantly improving. It's also important for salespeople to distance themselves from their competition and therefore demonstrate how much better they are from other sellers. Really, being competitive is table stakes for the sales profession.

A real-life example of work ethic and competitiveness was when I was hired from being an independent sales rep to working for that legitimate multinational company. My first day on the job I attended a sales meeting where I met the other sales reps and gained insight into the mindset of the team. Granted, they were pioneering a new brand in the USA with a steep price tag and an unorthodox way of going to market. However, the griping I heard was petty. Given where I came from and what I had endured as a full commission rep, they had no idea how lucky they were. One rep in particular who was at the top of the leaderboard was complaining that he was away from home an average of two and a half days a week. He also said he was going to crush his number that year and leave us all in the dust. There was no way I was going to let that guy beat me even though I still needed to be onboarded and get up to speed on some technical products.

My exposure to those sales reps at that meeting was probably one of the best things that ever happened to me. It really motivated me to push as hard as I could and completely dominate. This is where the combination of work ethic, competition, and grit create a winning formula. When my competition was resting, I was already working. When they were out having drinks, I was preparing for the week ahead. I put in the necessary work and sacrifice to get results. There were times when I wasn't home for seven weeks! There wasn't a month I wasn't away from home for at least two weeks. I squeezed in as much impactful activity as I possibly could, covering a lot of ground to ensure I missed nothing. I did the work of three reps and saw the fruits of my labor not just on the leaderboard, but also in my pay.

Looking back, those first couple of year end reviews were pretty funny. My boss and president of the subsidiary, a freakishly tall, soft-spoken German who looked menacing if you didn't know him, would recap the highlights of the year. Then we would get into an unusual debate on pay.

"You earned the maximum for your bonus, but because it is capped, we want to give you 10 percent more for the extra achievement."

"As much as I appreciate it, we had an agreement and I did my part, so no need to do anything different for me," I responded.

"This comes from the big Kahunas in Europe," he said. "They knew you would say that and they insist. You are setting the bar and it makes us happy to reward you above and beyond!"

"I'm happy for the opportunity, that's enough."

"Ok, I'm happy you are happy, so the additional bonus is going to be in your next check," he said. "Trust me, accept it, given what we have to do this year, the goals are very aggressive."

Honest to god, I swear on The Bible that the conversations went down like that. I feel compelled to make that pronouncement because when I mention this story people think I'm exaggerating. The extra money was nice, it helped to ease financial burdens but really, the acknowledgment was the true fruit of my labor and it is what charged me to continue to put out. That and handing everyone else their ass!

CHAPTER 2

Sales Pipeline

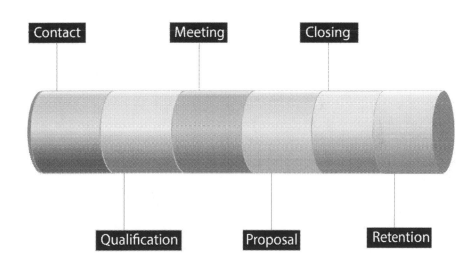

It was my first month as an independent sales rep, and I was riding with a coworker in his territory to get up to speed.

Jerry presented himself as a blues guitar playing straight shooter who wore snakeskin cowboy boots and a hat no matter the occasion. I would find out later he had a propensity to violate the first sales commandment and take on some of the traditional characteristics that have marred the sales profession. The drive from Phoenix to Flagstaff afforded plenty of opportunity for business conversations, and on our journey, Jerry kept throwing out terms and expertise to convey his seeming high sales caliber.

Jerry kept mentioning, "The pipeline . . ."

We sold thousands of different products, and I honestly didn't know what he was talking about. In a display of pure ignorance, I asked, "Are we selling plumbing materials too?"

Jerry looked at me oddly, "What do you mean?"

"You keep mentioning pipeline, and I'm confused as hell."

He giggled, shook his head, adjusted his hat, and said, "No, numb nut, the pipeline is made up of stages in the sales process."

Embarrassing moments like that tend to commit things to memory so they won't be repeated.

It may not seem obvious at a high level, but the sales profession is multifaceted. The digital world has forced the sales profession to evolve. For non-sales professionals, this chapter is designed to provide an understanding of the sales process.

For years I've had discussions with sales reps who were dissatisfied with their positions. Some were even considering changing their careers and moving out of sales, all without understanding their *actual* place in the sales pipeline!

What I've come away from after those discussions and my early naivete is how desperately people in the profession need this conversation.

I don't blame some of the dejected I've talked with over the years, those in particular who owned the entire sales pipeline, which is a traditional sales carryover. Conversely, the more complex the sale and the higher the potential revenue, the more likely the sales role is highly specialized and teams are segmented into major stages of the sales pipeline. There's good reason why companies that scale have an assembly line sales team structure that corresponds to the sales pipeline stages where specialized teams divide and conquer. Regardless of whether the sales team structure is an assembly line, POD, or Island, understanding the sales pipeline stages is a fundamental first step.

Note: For the sake of clarity, there's a difference between a sales pipeline and a sales funnel, though many naively use these terms interchangeably. The sales pipeline focuses on steps in the sales process, while the sales funnel focuses on the customer journey. When you hear that reps need to manage their sales pipeline, it usually means updating their CRM (customer relationship management software) and moving prospective customers to the next process step when possible. Full disclosure, there may be varied stages to the pipeline, depending on the product or service offering. I'm going to focus on just the most widely accepted and critical stages.

Sales Pipeline Stage I – Contact

The first step in the process is *contact*.

In a traditional sales environment, this would take the form of a cold call from a rep who owned the entire sales pipeline. The rep would literally open up this big directory book of contact information called the *Yellow Pages* and just start calling people cold who looked promising.

Today there are more savvy ways to generate what we call *warm* leads by pinging potential customers in some way to get them to show interest, be it through a sign up of a free online newsletter that reflects the company's product or service in some way, or a host of other ways—consider Search Engine Marketing (SEM) and to some degree Search Engine Optimization (SEO) possibly in the form of microsites. And then there is the world of third-party sales lead aggregators that use their platforms to pass along lead lists (for a price!) to companies that have a chance of converting these leads into actual sales.

Regardless of how they come in, sales leads need to be contacted, and that's the very first stage in the pipe. In this new sales era, someone called a Sales Development Rep (SDR) is usually tasked with reaching out to hundreds and even thousands of these potential customers every day. It also means following up, usually about seven times, which is typically the threshold of diminishing returns and badgering. There's a high volume at the front end of the pipe, and conversion to move the sale forward is extremely low. In fact, a 2 percent conversion rate is considered good. There are of course tactics on the growth or marketing side that can be employed to make these leads *hot* instead of *warm*, but that usually costs too much per lead or yields far fewer leads, which impacts Gross Market Volume (GMV), an important figure used in the investor pitch deck at startups.

The life of the SDR is a total grind. *Activity dominators* outperform everyone else, but staying motivated long term is tough even if you're at the top of the performance dashboard. Even for the grittiest, SDR's face *a lot* of daily rejection. In fact, that abuse is probably why, in an effort to attract more applicants, some sales job ads state that there is "no cold calling," though initial lead contact is still low conversion regardless of how *warm* leads actually are.

A good sales leader uses techniques to keep morale up and help out SDRs (more on this later in the book). Bottom line: contact is a necessary first step in the sales process, usually tasked by someone who is new to sales, new to the workforce, or is trying to break into a new industry.

Sales Pipeline Stage II – Qualification

The *qualification* stage is of vital importance. When done right, it increases revenue through sales acceleration. Conversely, unqualified leads clog the pipe and are expensive for the company, filling the rep workload with prospect chasing without realizing the fruits of the labor.

The tells for qualifying prospective customers should be data driven and aligned with the sales context of the business. They should also be easily repeatable. An effective methodology adopted by many progressive sales organizations is *lead scoring*, where prospects are objectively ranked for sales readiness using behavioral, firmographic, and demographic attributes.

Dedicated teams commonly focus on qualification these days, especially when inbound volume is high, the sales cycle is long, and consensus decision making is involved (more on that in a later chapter as well). If the sale is less complex, sales reps likely handle this stage and the rest, referring to the qualification activity as the *qual call*. Regardless of structure, the purpose is to prioritize leads based on the likelihood of converting leads to customers. Then you either disqualify, de-prioritize, or advance to the next stage.

Sales Pipeline Stage III – Meeting (and Discovery)

The *meeting* stage is a sort of catchall.

Normally, several meetings are required unless the sale is strictly transactional. In those instances, phone calls or phone meetings may be sufficient. Until the recent past, getting face-to-face meetings was the goal. With the widespread adoption of technology, video calls and live chats have taken over, making it more convenient since everyone in the meeting can be remote, and less expensive since travel isn't required.

Face-to-face meetings are still best, especially when it's a consensus sale and large amounts of capital are on the line. Although video calls may help to a point with deciphering body language, currently nothing takes the place of in-person meetings and the personal dynamic they encourage.

Given the global economy, budget restrictions for travel, and everyone's increasingly busy schedules, there is developing technology working to address this need and combine the benefits of remote video call meetings and face-to-face meetings. At the vanguard of this effort is Mimesys, which uses spatial co-presence technology to put everyone in the meeting in the same room using a holographic replica of each participant. For the techie, Mimesys uses volumetric telepresence for real time communication and collaboration. If you're thinking of something you've seen from *Star Wars*, you're not far off. But the experience is even more realistic due to spatial awareness[iv].

The term *discovery* is associated with the initial meeting since it is investigative. After listening intently to the customer's needs, Sales Reps test the waters, throwing out some potential solutions to see if the client is interested. This is also a time when potential *cross selling* and *upselling* is identified. There may be brief follow up meetings, where explanations and deliverables are provided by the client.

In all these meetings it's paramount to remember the sales commandments we've covered so far. Too often sales reps "show up and throw up" with their company brand and offering without stopping to listen first. It's amateur hour when reps talk themselves out of the sale.

Remember we have two ears and one mouth. We should be listening twice as much as we speak as sales professionals. I understand the motivation to over-talk since getting the appointment takes a lot of effort and a rep wants to perform to close the sale. The most successful reps know that their *sales pitch* must be tailored to the customer's needs and that will not happen unless the customer tells you what those needs are first.

Sales Pipeline Stage IV – Proposal

Successful sales reps take the information gleaned during discovery and follow up meetings to come back with a prescriptive solution for their product or service. Sadly, having the sale "die on the vine" here is not uncommon.

A variety of factors may kill the sale, such as momentum loss because of time delay to turnaround on the *proposal*, having a new decision maker get involved, having a decision maker already involved in the process not in consensus, realizing the budget is allocated for something else, or discovering the proposal is completely *tone deaf*, meaning the reps really didn't listen to the customer's needs and are just selling a cookie cutter product or service that doesn't fit. For whatever reason, when the prospective customer goes dark after all that effort, it's very frustrating. Regardless of the cause, the rep needs to go back up the sales pipeline one stage and perform some thorough fact finding before revising the proposal. That's the best-case scenario here. It's more likely the rep needs to move back up the pipe even further to qualification for good measure. The sale may be salvaged, but if the root cause for the sale not moving forward can be identified it serves as a lesson learned for the sales reps to be more effective in the future, while also bringing the relationship closure.

If the previous meeting stage in the pipe was diligent, then the client accepts the proposal. Well, sort of… They indicate they accept it, but they usually want more for less before committing. Enter negotiation and a subset of the next stage in the sales pipeline.

Sales Pipeline Stage V – Closing

The term *closing* is a bit misleading on the surface, especially among the uninitiated. Closing the sale equals getting the sale. And for those self-promoting sales reps, the sale isn't closed until the client has made the actual transaction!

Before that happens, negotiation occurs. Everyone is near the finish line. Reps are salivating, but the power rests squarely with the buyer, and they know this. So, the buyer asks for discounts, more features for the same price, or favorable payment terms. The reps take custom steps to give the customer something more but not everything the customer asks because that's bad negotiation and leaves the customer feeling like they should have asked for even more. In the end there's middle ground, and the customer commits to the purchase.

Sales Pipeline Stage VI – Retention

Retention is the final stage and commonly overlooked unless the customer has only purchased part of the product or service.

It's easier and less expensive to sell to existing customers than acquiring new ones—just imagine having to run though all the stages of the pipeline with new folks again. So why do reps skip this step or just skim over it?

One possibility: getting new customers diversifies a rep's client portfolio and builds their territory. So, on one hand they're financially incentivized to hunt for new customers more than grow existing business. They also get excited with the prospect chase. Or perhaps they want to avoid customers expressing dissatisfaction with the products or services provided and paid for already.

Whatever the motivation, customer retention is important for the sales rep and for the business in order to maximize *customer lifetime value*. In other words, this step needs to be followed methodically. For sales reps adept at customer retention, a solid list of active references will emerge that can be used to secure new customers in the future.

So here we are post-closing. The customer has just made the purchase. After the customer has had a chance to experience the product or service, the rep needs to check-in with them. And don't just send a half-assed survey from your company. You, as the rep, need to speak to a decision maker and ask for candid feedback. Were they happy or dissatisfied? Where were expectations exceeded, and where did they fall short? Sales reps need to show they care about the customer and that the relationship goes much deeper than that first purchase.

When done right, the rep will have built rapport and there will be openings for further selling. This creates a shortcut in the sales pipeline, or a truncated pipe, if the same actors are involved. In such an instance, the pipe will restart at *discovery*, stage three.

Positioning Yourself in The Pipeline

Having a good understanding of the sales process now, I'd like to circle back to those disgruntled sales reps I mentioned at the beginning of the chapter.

I know what it's like to own the entire pipeline end to end. You have to know your product and service inside out, *and* you have to be a jack of all trades (and master of none) along the way. With such a demanding set up, it's hard to be effective even part of the time. Company founders, or very early stage companies where total employees don't even fill in the seats at the kitchen table, may not have another choice, though.

However, once there has been proof of concept and an actual sales team exists, owning the entire pipeline is counterproductive and unnecessary. Sales reps who find themselves owning the entire pipeline at later-stage companies simply need to get out. Life is easier and more effective with stage specialization structures.

It's no secret that sales reps are money motivated, some more so than others. If you were to advise one of these mercenary sales reps on what pipeline stage to try to land a job in, what would you say?

One way to think of it: the closer a position is to actually *making* the sale happen, the *more* the rep can command from their employer. Sales professionals at the front end of the pipeline get paid substantially less than those at the tail end of the pipeline who have the most influence on getting the sale closed for the company and moving the revenue needle.

So then why do sales professionals list front-of-pipeline activities in their resumes and LinkedIn profiles? Unless they're sourcing for SDRs, hiring managers don't care if a rep called one hundred new accounts a week. Heck they can have someone in Asia do that for pennies per call at ten times the volume. However, if the rep changes that description to "brought in twenty new accounts," or "added new accounts to grow territory 25 percent YoY," that resonates and conveys the rep belongs near the more lucrative tail end of the pipe.

That brings us to the next logical question. What job title should that sales rep be using in the job board search function to narrow down open positions?

By the end of the next chapter, you'll be able to answer that question as we explore different sales job titles, what they mean for different businesses in different industries, and how this knowledge will empower you to recognize the skills a rep brings to an organization.

CHAPTER 3

Decoding Sales Titles

It was a stellar New Year and the forecast was looking good as we watched the procession of sales professionals gather in the Las Vegas conference center. The main product line at our rep agency was expanding, and hopes were soaring. They had successfully acquired two companies with recognized brands and brought in all the sales reps from the country for a national sales meeting.

The auditorium was decorated with new brand colors, and the number one everywhere. Amidst the cacophony of reps, I turned to Bob and asked, "What do the ones mean?"

Reps around us stopped to listen.

"Stevie, my boy, I hope it's not our new commission," said Bob with a giggle.

"The power of one!" A short and stout product manager from a newly acquired company chimed in. "The theme of the meeting," he said, walking toward the podium where shortly thereafter he attempted to introduce himself to the audience.

As the product manager spoke, Tom, who was sitting next to me, cupped his hands around his mouth and shouted, "Stand up!"

The same call echoed from different pockets of the auditorium, until a few groups were chanting in unison, "Stand up, stand up!"

The vertically challenged product manager's face was red with embarrassment as he stood on his toes, still barely reaching over the podium. He responded colorfully, to which the crowd erupted in laughter.

An intense, bowtie-wearing executive with white hair parted to the side walked on stage and delivered a speech then, confirming the theme. He was the VP of Sales and Marketing for the parent company of all these brands. Emphasizing how we would all integrate as "one" moving forward, he then gave us what he said was really good news.

"We are issuing all of you new business cards, and with them new titles," he said. "Effective immediately you are no longer sales reps. Going forward you are Marketing Managers!"

Bob turned to me and said, "Look at that Stevie, on the job only a couple of months and you already got a promotion!"

The news wasn't exactly as grand as it sounded.

The caveat to this chapter is that sales titles should be considered within the context of the business where the sales professionals work. The topic is a rabbit hole. For nearly every position I have listed in **Appendix I**, one can find job descriptions online that tell another story.

Add to that that sometimes titles among sales professionals are meaningless, and the picture gets even murkier. Take the VP of Sales title. It should refer to someone with the responsibility to shape sales infrastructure, lead all the different layers of direct reports in sales, and be responsible to execute on the company's growth objectives through the sales force. For a startup making its first sales hire, the VP of Sales is probably the first sales rep and an individual contributor, and they usually own the entire sales pipeline.

Using the VP of Sales title to hire frontline sales reps works because it attracts more applicants, even if the position is nowhere near the senior management level where it should be. I've known salespeople in the United States who have taken pay *haircuts* to work in identical roles for other companies because of the seemingly prestigious title of VP of Sales.

As Americans, I think we're infatuated with titles. Therefore, an entire chapter needs to be devoted to looking at the topic honestly, without manipulation or ego attached.

Blinded by Title Love

When I was VP of Sales for a multinational company, my counterparts in France, the United Kingdom, the Netherlands, and elsewhere had the title of National Sales Manager or Managing Director. Okay, sure, my sales organization was bigger and the market was larger, but all of our responsibilities were similar. Yet I had VP tagged onto my name. Like I said, we Americans love our titles!

An argument can be made, and usually is, that a flashy title gives more credibility for meeting with prospective customers. I've found this holds water with conflict resolution more so than in prospective customer meetings.

A top sales rep from my staff was offered the opportunity to be the first rep to sell a sister company's product line. The focus was on the U.S., though there was no coverage in all of North and South America, so the territory was flexible. Furthermore, as their inaugural rep for the region, he was able to choose his own title, which he did, a version of North and South America Sales Manager.

I asked him why he stopped short there. He should have just gone full bore and said he was in charge of the Western Hemisphere! Mind you, he had no direct reports, no influence on strategy, no structural impact on sales operations, and only a spattering of customers, the vast majority of whom were in the U.S. But he argued that he did have B2B customers as far south as Brazil that he had to "manage" (sales professionals can justify anything).

Being mindful that titles are not always what they seem, **Appendix I** contains a breakdown of some common sales titles and descriptions.

The variation in sales title definitions and pay fluctuate considerably not only across industries with different products/services and sales cycles, but also within the same industry, depending on growth phase of the company and many other factors such as years of experience and level of education depending on the role. For these reasons, high level buckets are the most reliable way to break down some of the most popular sales roles. Drawing on experience, an internal survey, and data from the U.S. Bureau of Labor Statistics, the following matrix is an attempt to shed some light on different sales roles across industries.

Title	Seniority Level	Compensation Plan	Comments
Sales Representative	Individual Contributor	Typically low base/ high commission

The pay distribution range varies greatly from approximately $40,000 to approximately $170,000 | Industries with consumable products and transactional sales earn much less than consultative solution selling of software, medical devices, or financial instruments. Geography influences pay; e.g., salespeople in NYC earn more. |
| **Account Executive** | Individual Contributor | Low base/ high commission

Approximately $120,000 per year   on average | Product/service, industry, deal size, and market influence compensation. |
| **Sales Development Rep** | Individual Contributor | Hourly plus bonus

Approximately $30,000 a year on average | Industry, product/ service, long/short sales cycle and market influence compensation. |
| **Regional Sales Manger** | Individual Contributor | 70 percent salary to 30 percent variable pay

Approximately $80,000 a year on average | Industry, product/service, long/short sales cycle and market influence compensation. |

Title	Seniority Level	Compensation Plan	Comments
Sales **Manager** (or Regional Sales Manager with direct reports)	Low	2/3 base to 1/3 variable Approximately $100,000 a year on average	Sales cycle, product/ service, industry, and market influence compensation.
Sales **Director**	Middle	High base plus variable Approximately $130,000 a year on average	Sales cycle, product/ service, industry, and market influence compensation.
VP of Sales	Senior	High base plus bonus Approximately $200,000 a year on average	Company size, number of direct reports, ARR, industry, product/service influence compensation.
Chief Sales Officer	Executive	High base plus bonus Approximately $250,000 a year on average	Company size, ARR, industry, product/service influence compensation.

Based on the previous matrix, here is what an organizational chart might look like:

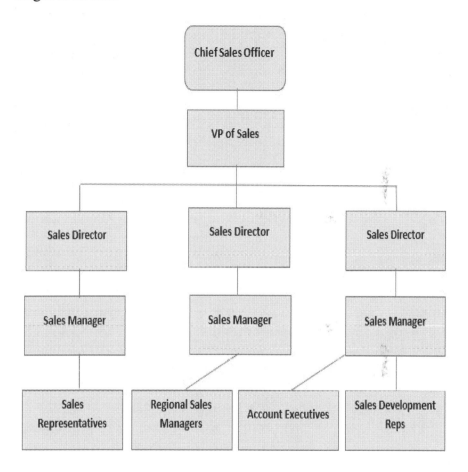

Let's circle back to the question at the end of the previous chapter.

Given the titles and descriptions you just read, if you were to advise someone who wanted to be in an individual contributor sales role with the "largest upside" (sales talk for most lucrative), which single title would be best fitted?

Note: Answer at the end of the chapter.

I Want to be Paid What I'm Worth!

Who doesn't? The question is, what are you *really* worth?

Too many times to count, I've heard sales reps say they want to get paid what they are worth. Reasonable enough. That is until expectations become unreasonable.

For example, one rep who owned the entire pipeline for a provision business said he needed to earn at least $250k a year to be paid what he was worth. Mind you, he was a recent college graduate and had only been in sales for a few years.

I asked how he reached that figure? He said that was what he needed to survive, to which I replied he was conflating what he was worth with what he desired.

Let's break down that rep's desire using back of the envelope math. Companies generally calculate for a minimum return of three times what they pay their outside sales reps. That number covers the costs of the rep, plus overhead, marketing/lead generation, and any off-the-menu costs that can be assigned to that rep.

That means this rep would have needed to bring in a minimum of $750k to $1M in gross sales revenue per year (or more) just as a break even. If reps aren't paying for their own compensation plus expenses, they're usually let go after a year, though the compensation incentive plan should be designed to protect the company and incentivize the rep to hit the expected revenue objectives (more on this in a latter chapter).

Was this rep meeting those numbers right out of college? You guessed it. Not even close.

What Are You Worth?

It's a good exercise to be able to justify your worth, regardless if you are in sales or in another profession. It becomes particularly important if you are in sales, where decisions often break down to numbers at day's end.

There are a variety of creative ways to do this. The most rudimentary: start with how many gross sales dollars you brought in during your most recent best year. Then divide by three. Warning: you may be disappointed with the answer.

Conversely, it may *not* be an accurate calculation for different types of business to use this simple method, especially if the sales rep is in a role where they own only part of the pipe or where there is an established territory with top accounts. A safe bet for figuring value that's difficult to dispute is to take true contributions (new account totals, increased dollars over last year from existing accounts) and anything else you can prove you had a direct contribution in revenue to for the company, and then extrapolate a figure from that.

By the way, using these facts and figures is a great way to get on the same page as the head of finance and assists your boss in making the arguments for a pay increase on your behalf. Come armed with figures that show how much is contributed to the company. Support your numbers with facts like hours worked, select milestone accomplishments that helped the company, and bell-weather examples of future sales performance. These are all great ways to negotiate for higher pay.

In sales, unlike like many other functions, the added area of negotiation is in bonus earnings. I have yet to find a CFO who was opposed to structuring a compensation package so the reps have the potential to earn more if they are superstars. What the CFO wants to avoid is leaving money on the table. So, if the rep exceeds revenue expectations, the rep will benefit financially. It may mean less base salary, but if reps are confident in their abilities, they will take that risk to earn a lot more.

How to Sell Yourself

Each sales title carries a responsibility of value for the organization. If it didn't, the position wouldn't exist. Sales professionals that zero in on that ability, really identifying what brings the company the most value, are the ones who successfully sell themselves. They also support that value-creating ability with anecdotal evidence and are capable of weaving it into the conversation in a manner that sounds modest rather than arrogant.

For example, if ABC Company is hiring for a field sales position, as a sales rep, how do you set yourself apart? When they ask what makes you different from others (and they will), it's a chance to convey that you make the company money, lots of money.

You might say: "Since taking over my territory it has grown 126 percent on average, and I've brought in $4M in new revenue. My product knowledge and customer service has allowed me to have a 93 percent retention rate, while new customer acquisition has grown on average 50 percent a year."

If the position is geared more towards new business, then a deep dive with examples on hunting for new accounts would be appropriate. Highlight and pinpoint some of the hard-working and creative tactics you used to achieve those goals as well. Conversely, if growing the existing customer base through cross selling activities is called out in the job description, that's the area to go deep on.

At the end of the day the prospective company is taking a risk with a hire, and everyone involved in the hiring process wants to be reassured that you'll not only meet the requirements for the position and be a fit, but that you'll thrive in order to set new benchmarks. Your success is their success. You should leave no doubt in their minds.

A Note on Inside (Call Center) Versus Outside (Field) Sales

There's a big difference between inside sales and outside sales.

To be a successful outside salesperson requires a lot of the skills and discipline found with the successful inside salesperson. However, outside sales, where face-to-face meetings are required, has lower volume, higher stakes, and greater autonomy to get the sale. It also means working long hours, traveling, often working weekends, attending tradeshows, and a host of other events to get in front of customers and to hone skills.

Inside sales is more process-driven, with high volume and predictable work schedules. Customer outreach is conducted through the phone (*VoIP*) and email. Many inside sales professionals admit they need to have someone holding them accountable, and someone to ensure they are following process. The opposite is generally the case with outside sales professionals who value their flexibility and rely on their own discipline to work hard daily to hit goals to grow their territories.

By the way, the answer to the question on which sales role and title would be most lucrative is Account Executive (AE). See **Appendix I** on the definition of an AE.

CHAPTER 4

Best Practices

Whether you are a front-line sales rep, in sales leadership, or a coworker in a non-sales role, this section is for you.

For the sales rep, this section contains actionable insights. For sales leaders, it serves as a reminder to hold sales reps accountable in order to reinforce fundamentals essential for performance. For those in non-sales roles, it will provide you with the knowledge to be able to identify which sales reps in your organization are doing the right fundamental things and which are not.

So, let's get started!

Sales professionals should think of themselves as firefighters, because inevitably things go astray, and we have to put out the fires. Actually, sales professionals use the phrase "putting out fires" frequently to refer to handling issues that may derail a sale, addressing customer complaints, or any host of internal or external issues impeding sales performance.

While the metaphor is long established, it turns out there are actually some important lessons sales professionals can really learn from firefighters. If you've ever been to a fire station or seen inside the compartments of a fire engine, the first thing you might notice is the high level of organization.

The fire apparatus is organized with labeled compartments that house the essentials required during an emergency. Specific compartments have mounted hand-held fire extinguishers, hand tools, electrical equipment, salvage gear, adapters/nozzles/fittings, and hoses. Mounted to the inside doors of compartments are each firefighter's self-contained breathing apparatus (SCBA). Under duress, mitigating the chaos by having the things needed in an organized manner provides some control of the situation and sets up the team for success. Any firefighter can intuitively go to the correct compartment to get the necessary object needed for the application in an emergency.

Regardless of whether sales reps work in call centers or the field, I've seen over the years that those leading their fields are, without exception, clearly organized. On the inside it meant they had a clear and organized desk. They had a crib sheet in place to reference for emergencies, and they were generally prepared with information on hand should they need it at a moment's notice. In the field, products were well maintained with replaced consumables so they could be demonstrated at their best. Marketing collateral was organized in folders. Resource information was on hand, and additional supplies for common repairs were available in a specific compartment (hero kit). When I was a sales rep, I kept a portable cabinet in my trunk that contained all the paperwork from each account in my territory (even easier now with everything digitized and accessible through a laptop or smartphone). Too many times to count being able to reference paperwork I had on hand made the difference between getting the sale on the spot and delaying or losing the sale altogether.

At the daily level, being organized makes reps more efficient. So be organized. It's the smart and sensible play. Sales reps who are clearly disorganized are waving a major red flag to clients, customers, and their company. When the inevitable happens and an upset customer has an emergency, who is best suited to handle the situation—the organized or disorganized rep?

Planning is a huge component of organization. For the inside sales rep, this may include having a target list of customers to reach out to throughout the day, appointments scheduled in the calendar, or even a block of time designated to follow up. For the outside sales rep, it means all these things plus planning the routes for the week.

Field reps should treat route planning as though they were full commission reps and had to pay for their own vehicle-related expenses. That mindset forces the rep to be more efficient in their route planning.

In the field reps sometimes have to work around traffic, appointment availability, and road congestion. This underscores the importance of being organized and planning the route carefully, including having time buffers in case there are unexpected delays. With real time traffic updates available through our smartphones, modifying routes has never been easier. But nothing takes the place of having the route planned out in the most-efficient manner to begin with.

Organization also takes the form of meeting preparation. Speaking from personal experience, as well as my observations with best-in-class sales reps, a tremendous amount of time is spent preparing. Usually an entire office day for the appointments during the week is not enough. Office days are controversial; many sales leaders want their reps in the field, but being deliberate about office days makes a lot of sense. This means not only concentrating on the necessities for each meeting, but also when to take the office day.

Being one of twenty-six subsidiaries worldwide, we had some very smart people based in Europe who did a detailed analysis of traffic patterns and found that the best day to take office days was Fridays. Many reps start their week taking an office day on Monday, but the data shows that is a mistake. Picking the right day and doing the right things during office days pays dividends.

Working when other reps are typically absent is a great way to stand out and build rapport with customers. You'll also garner mad respect in the company and profession. These are the people who really grind that we spoke of earlier. It may be as simple as making account visits on Mondays. It may be working days or even seasons that scarcely are worked by competitors. Whatever the way, put the extra time in to stand out.

As a sales rep with a large territory (half the known world as one friend put it), I opened an account in Alaska. It turned out to be a great account. In fact, they were in the top 25 percent of all my accounts, edging out the majority of those in the contiguous states I covered. I have to confess that I was advised not to open this account by my boss. I promised that my expenses would more than be offset by the revenue they brought in, and I argued that we needed to plant our flag in that territory to keep competition at bay.

In order to keep my promise, I became extremely sensitive to keeping my costs down while still doing what it took to make this account a success. It just so happens that the best time for a sales rep to go to Alaska and keep costs down is the middle of the winter, late January and into early February before the Iditarod. Overall travel costs are the lowest. The owner of my account said I was the first sales rep they had seen during the winter, and that reps usually come up in the summer, when they spend an hour or two working and the rest of their days on vacation. Later they said they trusted me from the start because they "knew I was for real" and looking after their best interests when I showed up in the middle of winter.

Truth be told, they were among my most prepared accounts. They were always prepared: events set up, end user calls ready, trainings planned and primed. You name it and they did maximize my time and grow their sales and profit. Looking back on it now, it makes a lot of sense to be prepared if you live in Alaska, where the lead time for supplies is long and being without essentials jeopardizes survival. As an aside, it's hard for me to think of better people than these folks in Alaska who treated me like family, taking me to their private cabin in the wilderness, having me attend local hockey championships where I watched the best hockey game of my life. The game went into over-time, passed through a shoot-off stalemate, and then into sudden death, where the team that a staff member from my account was on won in the end with his shot. It was also the game where that staff member bit off a big portion of his tongue and after sent me next-day delivery, fresh-caught succulent king crab. My point: when you build trust and are sincere about helping customers, they will treat you like family.

Following Through Matters

Follow-through is part of organization and planning, and it's a stand-out characteristic of effective sales reps.

In the most basic sense, follow-through is simply following up on your commitments, such as circling back with a deliverable that was promised to the customer (before the customer asks again for it), or getting back to a coworker. It also means being persistent: following up to check on the status of the sale to move it down the pipeline or keep it on hold.

After years in sales, following up has become an ingrained trait for me. That's the goal, really. Whether I'm following up daily as a sales professional, or with friends and family in my personal life, I do so almost automatically. Strive for that level in your work and life as well.

When things fall through the cracks, they can be costly. It's your job to make money, not lose money, so guard gains at all costs.

Navigating the Maze of Internal Obstacles

Beyond the field and your customers, there are a host of internal obstacles that impact your mood and therefore your performance and ability to achieve those best practices we're all after.

Sales reps should set reminders, fill in calendars, do what it takes to ensure follow ups are handled methodically with internal staff who are probably overwhelmed with other responsibilities and need reminders. Good sales reps know the individual preference of communication within the organization. Sally, who handles C-accounts for the region in inside sales, may prefer email communication, while Ben, the sales director, expects his direct reports to text follow-ups so he can jump on them right away. Sales reps work with these folks every day, so remember to be careful with tone. Prefacing messages by saying they're a "friendly reminder" certainly helps, even if it's the fifteenth follow up.

Sales commandments four and six (having a winning attitude and grit) also apply to interaction with internal staff. Mistakes occur, unexpected issues arise. People drop the ball. It happens. Sales reps need to be respectful, understanding, and above all stay positive.

A note on gossip, another scourge of internal environments: just don't. Gossip tends to take on negative narratives. Negative narratives strain relationships. Sales reps should stay away from speaking about others unless it's strictly positive. Just as clients are treated professionally, sales reps should treat internal staff professionally as well. Gossiping leads to no good for anyone.

Selling Yourself: The Necessity of *Selling Up!*

Some of the best salespeople have been passed over by others who were really only proficient at selling themselves.

I've done this for two decades, and I'm adamant that my results will speak for themselves. But boy did I work unnecessarily hard to get here. I was accused by my bosses of failing to self-promote, which I felt was insincere and wrong at the time. Years later I find myself advising the best sales professionals that put out the best work yet are too humble to be on the radar to *sell up*!

While I might seem a hypocrite on this topic, if I had a time machine, I'd probably take my own advice and put more effort into self-promotion. The argument can be made that upper management roles in many organizations aren't occupied by the most qualified people, but rather those who were able to convince the decision makers they were best for the roles or position.

You know what I'm talking about. Everyone has come across people in their workplace who hold an important, upper-management role they got because they were great at kissing up. Don't kiss up, by the way. That's *not* what I'm saying. Rather, sales reps should be sure people in the organization whose opinions count know of their hard-fought victories and good character.

Nowadays, nobody in executive leadership has the bandwidth to deep dive into the daily activities of sales reps to decipher these things (more on how front-line sales leaders can help in this regard later on in the book). So, the responsibility to sell up falls squarely on you, the sales rep, who should be looking for opportunities to shine in front of the boss's boss whenever possible.

This leads me to sales meetings, specifically level of engagement.

I'll be the first to admit that nobody likes someone at a sales meeting who just asks questions to appear to be smart or important. However, if the sales rep is truly engaged, and if the rep came prepared with the intent to satisfy curiosity, that benefits everyone and casts a positive light on the rep.

Curiosity is a strong sales trait to have. Curious people ask great questions, are engaged, and keep those around them on their toes. As mentioned previously, keep the conversation positive, respectful, and genuinely enjoy being around coworkers. You're all in the same boat, so you might as well help each other out.

The Not-So-Secret Superpower: Initiative

My final piece of best practice advice for sales reps is to take initiative to leverage resources. This ranges from having a product manager join an important call, to working with the head of service to satisfy a customer. It also means learning from the experts whenever possible, and constantly pushing to become better by learning from others.

When I was a full commission rep, I learned a lot from a product manager from a favorite product line. Mark was really smart. Like *really* smart. He knew his products, the market, the industry, and could sniff out bull a mile away. He was a big guy. Like *really* big. He had known the principals at our rep agency for many years, and they were extremely close. You could say too close actually.

The first time I met Mark we were in the conference room of the rep agency. Tom made some off-color remarks about Mark that made me uncomfortable. Mark fired back, and the entire exchange put me on edge even though they were laughing. Then Mark squeezed himself into one of the chairs. Within seconds, the chair fell apart and Mark came crashing to the floor. I was mortified and embarrassed for him.

Tom and Bob, now laughing, broke out in high fives, and I realized then they'd set a prank. Mark, though, was not laughing.

After a conversation that I won't dare repeat, we walked out to my compact, four-door sedan parallel parked in front of the rep agency building per Tom's request. Mark opened the door all the way, adjusted the seat as far back as it would go, and through trial and error, attempted to make his way in. The car was pitching and rolling as Mark struggled. I was trying to play it off like nothing unusual was happening. At this point Tom was outside laughing and taunting, while Mark was cursing his name as he struggled. To add insult to injury, the car had dipped considerably on the passenger's side. When Mark attempted to pull the door closed, it snagged on the high curb. Tom fetched Bob, and the two of them pushed the door closed, laughing hysterically as it scrapped the concrete. We started to pull away slowly while Mark flipped them the bird. Boy was I uncomfortable!

Mark could have said something derogatory about Bob and Tom. He would have had every right to. Instead, he just turned and said, "they're a lot of fun." He promised to give me something if we made a certain amount of sales that day. It seemed like a lofty goal, but I accepted the challenge. On the 90-minute ride to our first appointment, I learned a lot about some of the core products, how best to showcase them for B2B customers, and how to accurately read the price list for our different types of customers. Mark seemed more agitated with the fact that nobody had covered these fundamental things with me than the pranks from earlier.

At our first appointment, Mark wanted me to pitch the quarterly promotions. I did it as Tom did it with his accounts and quickly found out that I was doing it all wrong. Turns out the minimum purchase order combined with co-op advertising were required. Mark was gracious enough to wait until we got back into the car to chew me out.

At the end of it, though, he said he would approve the order without the requirement this one time only, but for the rest of the appointments that day he wanted me to take initiative and pitch the promos that were different for each account.

What I really appreciated was that he explained that the 10 percent or 15 percent discount being applied for the order was supposed to be to support marketing spend to grow the local business, and to raise the sales bar for that product category in the area in so doing. It wasn't for short-term customer profit like everyone else thought. The minimum order also made sense because it was supposed to last the entire quarter, although reorders were allowed so there wouldn't be a back-order situation.

Mark highlighted his expertise at every account we visited. The purchasing agents and owners immediately admired him. He seemed to know everything about their customers, the direction of their market, even about seemingly innocent subjects like sports. At every account, he asked them how I was doing, and had something positive to say about me. By the end of the day, with Mark's tutelage, I had secured a large amount of orders that exceeded our goal.

After, we were rushing to the airport to get Mark on the last Delta flight to Chicago. I didn't want him to miss his flight on my watch. And although he only had minutes to spare, when we arrived, pulling up to the departures curb, Mark opened his brief case and tucked a page from a newspaper under his arm before handing it to me.

"You have to promise me you will only use this when the time is right and you will never say you got it from me," he said.

I promised, and he handed me an article with a picture of a guy dressed like a monkey wearing an Angels' baseball jersey and being arrested in the outfield. Mark shook my hand, wished me luck, and said, "Tom monkeys around when he drinks."

Mark went to catch his flight, and I'll be if he didn't somehow make it.

That was the beginning of my true tutelage and when I began to understand the real value of both professionalism *and* initiative. When I was a rep, whenever I had someone ride with me, I did everything possible to learn from them. It was the fastest way to get better and gain expertise. My initiative and curiosity also endeared me to them, which was great when I was in a pinch and I needed help. Ultimately, I made more money and enjoyed the job more.

CHAPTER 5

Sales Tactics that Work

Basic sales tactics that become intuitive after repetitive implementation are oftentimes second nature for seasoned sales professionals. What's interesting is how curious non-sales personnel are in learning these tactics. Although this section is core to sales reps, it really can benefit everyone. Prepare to get into the weeds!

The Importance of Connection

We all have multiple interests. Complexities. Layers. Your potential customers are no different. When preparing for the meeting, phone call, or video chat, you need to identify a subject you can use to bond with your prospective customer that isn't business. Also, in the spirit of maintaining a positive mental attitude and transcending that into practice with customers, your common ground subject should preferably be something optimistic in nature. For example, if you identify that your prospect went to college in Indiana, and you spent time working there, be sure to strategically interject that into conversation.

You might say, "Based on your profile from the company website, it looks like you went to IU. Did you spend much time there other than college?" You have broken the ice and gotten the customer comfortable talking. Then explain how you can relate to the people, customs, environment, and what you miss most: "I miss the warm and genuine people there the most, great to come across another Hoosier. . ."

Following a formal introduction, the small talk should last two to five minutes tops! Some reps find themselves deviating so far from the purpose of the meeting that they waste too much precious time breaking the ice. In the cases where the AEs are calling on the C-suite where time is at a premium, being respectful of time is paramount. Reps are typically adept at picking up on bonding subjects that act as ice breakers. They can often do so on the spot, even picking out sports team paraphernalia, family photos on the office desk, or awards on the conference walls. If there's little to go off during prep, or when meeting with multiple stakeholders, researching the latest positive trends in the community is a good back up option.

Mirror, Mirror

After breaking the ice with a common subject, it's crucial to solidify the connection. When people engage in harmonious conversation about common subjects, they have a tendency to reflect each other. Physically, they sit or stand the same way, folding an arm and holding their chin while speaking and listening. They speak at the same pace and similar tone. They repeat each other's phrases and words. Abundant proof of this phenomenon is easy to observe by people watching in a social setting.

In a business environment, especially when the relationship is nascent, the technique to solidify the bond is *mirroring*. Over video conference or in person, reflecting similar body language does the trick. If the customer speaks with the hands, the sales professional should be physically expressive as well. Reflect their style or demeanor. Are they formal or casual, all about business or more relationship oriented? Their disposition should be immediately evident when face to face and apparent over the phone by paying attention to tone and vocabulary.

Over the phone, mirroring the customer's tone, speed, and volume is even more important than in person since body language reflection isn't an option. If the customer is well articulated, sales professionals should be articulate. When the customer speaks more simply, sales professionals should reflect that level of vocabulary to avoid talking down. Speed is just as important; don't be a fast-talking salesperson unless your customer is equally fast talking. Like a two-part epoxy, the common subject acts like the resin and mirroring acts like the hardener to form an unbreakable bond.

From the start of the conversation reps should be deliberate about conversation etiquette and listening. I know I'm beating a dead horse here with the listening theme. Just know there's a reason silent and listen share the same letters. Thankfully there's a technique that addresses intentional listening with talking over the other person. Visualize a pour over coffee pot where the liquid is flowing through the mesh filter holding the coffee grounds. Wait until that very last drop, suspended momentarily in air, drips into the liquid below. To apply that visualization to sales, wait until the customer is finished with the last word they are saying, then give it a second to process in your brain, before beginning to speak.

During your initial conversation and later, you'll find cues to creating positive ripple effects in the conversation. Think of your words like pebbles being thrown in a pond. It's important not to   take the bait on a digressive topic that can send the dialog down the rabbit hole and derail the purpose of the meeting. Once those cues are identified, use common transition terms like those found in improv, such as, "yes, and . . ." and "by the way." The goal here is to keep the conversation flowing in the right direction, so create ripples by throwing out more supporting information to extend positive momentum. Lastly, start "collecting yeses" as your final added technique, and the conversation can be steered toward success!

Customer: We really liked the widget when it was much simpler because it would run faster and last a lot longer. I hear it's more expensive now with bells and whistles we don't need, and with it more complicated, it probably breaks down more frequently . . .

You: That's great that you liked the previous model widget. By the way, customers agree with you, that reliability and quick start was what they liked most. They say of those two, reliability was the most important, would you agree?

Customer: Yes. Just like us, those customers know that you are stress free when you trust that widget not to breakdown when you are miles away in the field. It definitely makes your life easier to be able to rely on it.

You: Yes, and market research indicates there is a need for those other features, so we redesigned the widget to include those improvements. Engineers were tasked to maintain the same reliability as the previous model. If the new version was guaranteed to be just as reliable would you consider buying another?

Customer: Yes.

You: We want our customers to be happy, so we will repair or replace your new unit if it breaks down within warranty, which is based on extreme use in industrial applications. Can I put you down for one?

At this point, and whenever asking a closing question, use silence as a conscious technique. Wait until the customer responds, when that last drop from the coffee filter lands, before saying or doing anything further. If you speak immediately after asking a question, you're talking over the other person. If you have just asked for the sale and you continue to talk, you will literally talk yourself out of the sale. Give the other side a chance to process an answer without creating any distractions, and you should be golden! Nobody listens themselves out of a sale, so stay silent and motionless.

Customer: Yes.

Positivity and the Total Picture

Zeroing in on the positive, as minute as it may be, is key when selling internally and externally. Sales is influence and being strategic in influencing the conversation is key.

Here's a quiz on putting it all together. In the below piece of dialog, what statement should be highlighted, and how would you transition it into conversation?

Monday's really suck! I'm usually buried in emails, the calendar is full of back-to-back meetings, I'm living on coffee because I don't have time for lunch. At least my coworkers are going through the same thing, but it definitely doesn't make any of us look forward to getting to work on Monday . . .

Your answer should go something like this: "Yes, and at least your coworkers are in it together with you. All that effort on Mondays, it sounds like it sets a productive tone for the week. I would imagine that once it's over you and your coworkers are relieved and feel like you have made progress together towards your goals."

Bottom line, pick the nugget that influences the conversation in the direction you desire.

Clarifiers

It's easy to get so caught up listening for the sale that the customer gets the feeling they aren't being genuinely heard. That may not only kill the sale, it will kill rapport for any potential sales in the future. In addition to proper use of body language, use *clarifiers* to focus in on exactly what your customer is saying.

- Can you say a little more about that?
- If I understand correctly, you . . .
- Here's what I'm hearing . . .
- Help me understand . . .
- For my own understanding . . .

Not only do clarifiers make people feel as though they're truly being heard, they confirm the accuracy of what you hear so you can offer the correct solution.

A Note on Pricing

"You want a better price? It will be at the expense of something else."

Customers should be made aware that there are tradeoffs when it comes to price. Discounts are a race to the bottom. The way to avoid price as a negotiation point is to sell to the gap; form a mental bridge in the customer's mind from the present state (where they are) to the future state (where they need to go), and then cast your product or service as the bridge. When a solution is appealing, discounts are irrelevant to closing the sale, so a customer asking for that discount will most likely still buy even if no discount is given.

Let's take a look at price more closely and see how it can play out in real life.

In the U.S., there has been a fear that discounts applied to premium products would diminish the equity of the company brand, particularly when products were sold through distribution, not direct to consumers. There are plenty of examples where *master distributors* sell products to consumers for less than regular distributors can buy them from the manufacturer. Short term that's good for the customers, but the brand is irreparably tarnished and product quality goes down, due partly to the resulting slim margins.

The company where I worked had been successful in Europe and elsewhere, becoming a performance leader even, but it was still reluctant to come to the USA. Why? Well, as one member of the Board put it, "It's like a Turkish bazaar!"

Americans are conditioned to buy on price, especially in the industry where this company sold products. With the size and potential of the market, the company entered North America cautiously, only selling directly to consumers in the beginning.

Enter me. It seems from the first day I was hired I was advocating for regular distribution, making nationwide distributors serve as micro warehouses for our products.

I'd argue the one thing Americans want more than discounts is instant gratification. Price discounting continued to be a seemingly insurmountable issue early on. We saw how businesses would undercut each other to take customers, leaving the product brands as profit margins as the casualties. To recover from a 10 percent drop in price, the business would need to sell 20 percent more. Discounting also sets a precedent for customers, who are therefore encouraged to wait to buy until there's a sale or discount.

A few of us studied premium companies out there, including a certain cutting-edge electronics brand named after a fruit, looking at how they were allowed to implement consistent pricing. A product line I had represented in the past that lost equity in their brand due to second step distribution implemented a brand equity program to reverse course.

Although it had been years since I'd worked with him, I reached out to Mark, and he connected us with the law firm that manufacturer used. After much research, many discussions with attorneys, and a strategic commitment that would inform what we did with promotions going forward, we preemptively implemented a brand equity program. We faced no shortage of criticism for doing the opposite of everyone else in the industry at the time. But my boss and the CFO had the guts to toe the line. Our distributors could now sell our premium products as long as they stayed consistent with our suggested retail price. They were expected to abide by our brand equity program. If they chose to deviate, and we learned they deliberately violated our brand equity program, we would terminate the business relationship. We lost some good distributors (and some not so good distributors) in the process, but the advantages far outweighed those losses.

As salespeople, it meant we could advocate predictable margins to our B2B customers, reassuring them that they would not be undercut on price by the competition. For B2C customers, there was no need to waste time shopping around; the exact product model in New York sold for the exact price regardless if it was in Los Angeles or Dallas. Discounts in the form of promotions were a function of the brand, ensuring pricing was consistent during a specified time in every market domestically. We had some B2B and B2C customers that accused us of being un-American, though they were in the minority, and many of them became our customers later anyway!

Negotiating on price was simply not on the table for salespeople anymore. They had to do their jobs and actually sell a product that was much more expensive than the product of our rivals, who were giving theirs away with discounts.

It was vindicating to work shows next to competitive brands where we would sell based on the merits of how our products addressed applications rather than how cheap they were that day. We constantly outsold the competition from top and bottom line revenue. Good times!

Negotiations

A fair amount of sales is doing the negotiation dance, even if price isn't the stumbling block. I'd be remiss if negotiation wasn't mentioned at least at a high level. There are books and courses dedicated entirely to the subject, so I won't attempt to create negotiation masters in a few paragraphs. What I will say: great negotiation is all around us, and for those of us who are visual learners, there is plenty we can pick up.

American Pickers is a documentary-style TV show still going strong after a decade [v]. Antique shop owners travel around the country in search of rare antiques and national treasures, sifting through countless piles of items to find their gems. Granted, those like me who appreciate American history, enjoy this program. Sales professionals like myself are actually more drawn to watching because of the negotiation and high-caliber salesmanship, though. The hoarding, well, not so much!

In any given episode there are several polished negotiation techniques at work. How do we know they work? Anyone who can go in cold to a prospect's residence and convince them to part ways with cherished items they've had for decades or even passed down for generations at a price that allows enough margin for resale is a great negotiator.

These pickers break the ice by securing the first buy and through their expression of interest in the hoarded antiques. The common bond? Well both the prospects and the pickers have a shared appreciation for the history of the item under consideration. There are many instances when prospects sell the pickers items of high value for much lower than market prices because the pickers have convinced them that the items will be shared with the public or will find a place in the right home or museum.

If you watch closely, you'll recognize good sales and negotiation techniques everywhere. Best Alternative to A Negotiated Agreement (BATNA), rapport building, disclosure of personal information, active listening, open ended questions, mutual gains, reciprocity, use of cooperative vocabulary, mirroring, anchoring, and asking for the sale are all negotiation techniques that can be observed in episodes of *American Pickers*. The show also highlights good use of emotion and pause. For example, when the pickers ask to buy an antique and the prospect throws out a price, the pickers may react emotionally to indicate it's too high. Also, they do a great job at using silence when asking for the item. In every episode I've seen, the pickers and the prospects part ways in a much better place than when they started, all parties are happy. That's good sales and great negotiation.

Using Math to Sell

When accurate numbers are used to convey a point, they cannot be disputed. The smaller the number, the more palpable it is for the prospect. I learned early on to "break it down to the ridiculous." What sounds more palpable? Spending $1,188 per year, $99 a month, $22.85 a week, or $3.25 a day?

Unlike his father, my son loves golf. Unless there are windmills and castles, you probably won't find me on the golf course. Also, unlike his father, my son is mathematically minded. He brought to my attention that there's a program called *Youth on Course*, where participating golf courses allow kids to play for $5 a round. He didn't sell it that way, though. Instead he said it would cost "only 28 cents a hole"

($0.28 x 18 holes = $5). He could have gone another direction, instead calculating annual cost based on an average of once a week of play ($5 x 52 weeks = $260), but the kid knew I couldn't possibly say no to pennies.

The inverse is true when proving value. If I were advocating for my local golf course to become a participating member of *Youth on Course*, I would aim to use the largest possible numbers. I might say that kids seldom play all eighteen holes, often likely play less than nine, are likely to be accompanied by a full price paying adult and are exposed to golf clubs and attire they will rapidly go through as they grow every time they come into the pro shop. This is where customer lifetime value comes in, and that $0.28 becomes thousands of dollars for the golf course.

So, sales professionals, use math to your advantage! Associating the cost of a product or service into manageable chunks assists in eliminating the price barrier. Summing up the total value illustrates profit potential.

Just remember to break it down to the ridiculous, and always double check your math!

Selling Versus Telling

The core traits of a good salesperson—belief, conviction, and enthusiasm—should be harnessed for good.

The problem is that many sales professionals are information regurgitators. Telling is ineffective. "This is the perfect product for you!" is a phrase likely to get you nowhere fast when it comes to sales.

However, turning a statement into a question transforms telling into selling, and selling wins the day!

Consider this reframe. "Of the biggest problems you have, which three do you wish would disappear?" Weave questions into the conversation to move the sale forward and avoid leaving meetings feeling like customer interrogations.

Now that's selling.

Objections and Rebuttals

Objections are opportunities to open the door to the sale. As long as they're not confrontational, that is. When dialogue turns adversarial, everyone loses.

Instead follow a process that diffuses the potential for conflict.

Validate the objection. Is it a smokescreen or a legitimate objection? Respectfully look for the root cause of the objection.

Get agreement to continue the dialog. Salespeople that overstep boundaries and jump into forcefully selling at this point, run the risk of being seen in the same lens as traditional overbearing high-pressure salespeople from the past. Instead get agreement to continue before starting.

Go in for the sell.

Here it is in practice:

Customer: We're not ready now, may be in Q1 of next year.

You: (1) May I ask what makes Q1 better timing?

Customer: We will have a better understanding of how we will finish the year, what to allocate for next year's budget, plus this year's budget is already committed for and approved by the Board.

You: Okay. That makes sense. (2) We do have something on that if you will allow me.

Customer: Sure, go ahead.

You: (3) We can structure it so that you can benefit using the widget immediately, without paying until Q1 of next year. That solves the administrative obstacle and is more aligned with your buying protocol. If I give you favorable payment terms, will that earn your business?

Exhibitions, Tradeshows, and Open Houses

There I was at one of my first distributor's customer appreciation days. My makeshift booth comprised of a couple of tables with products I was demonstrating was eclipsed by the semi-trucks and elaborate booth configurations of my competitors that occupied most of the parking lot. My boss walked up to me after I did several demos with a product, successfully making a sale.

He pointed to a consumable piece that I kept reusing. "While I appreciate you saving the company money, that plastic insert only costs us 15 cents. Better to replace it every time you demo that product rather than lose the sale to save 15 cents."

Lesson learned on saving pennies when I should have been chasing dollars.

The lesson goes much further, of course. Products, whether they're hand-held machines or software, should be presented in their most pristine condition. They should show no signs of wear, be void of bugs, and be prepped to perform at their highest caliber. This is particularly important for high-end products; premium products should be presented as such, so they better look and function better than anything else around.

More times than not, products become static visual aids when the rep should put them through their paces and then explain the benefits to specific applications that were just demonstrated.   Most times, reps just talk, and talk . . . and talk, rather than show!

I learned this early on from the trainer at the multinational company where I was working. Bernie was uncomfortable with his English, so he would run the products in front of customers and just gesture at how the features and application benefits tied in. Customers bought, and he drew in a crowd at each show without exception.

Drawing in a crowd is an important tactic for many reasons, not least of which is *behavioral contagion*. There's a herd mentality of sorts that subconsciously influences us to investigate what's drawing a crowd. People gravitate towards where other people are showing interest. So, if you can exhibit in a way that highlights products and services *and* draws a crowd, success is nearly a foregone conclusion.

Really, though, the behavior of the rep has the greatest influence on the success at customer shows. Customers want unique experiences at these shows, something they couldn't experience at home buying online or when shopping locally like they usually do. Having marketing collateral on a table with a video playing in the background is a wasted opportunity and unlikely to draw a crowd. I've seen plenty of that, as well as reps sitting at the back of their booths reading newspapers (in the past) and scrolling through their phone (present). Reps need to make eye contact (take off those sunglasses and put those phones away) with customers in the aisle and give them a reason to step into their booth.

Moments before writing this section I was at a local farmer's market. About two thirds of the booths had no customers. Meanwhile, the reps were in the back looking at their phones. The third of booths with reps who were engaging customers were drawing people in and making sales. All the while, prospective customers were walking through the market passing on some nice local goods because the exhibitors weren't making an effort. It was hard to understand. If the reps were going to be there anyway, why not make the best of it, engage with customers, and push for some sales?

In planning shows, reps like me would work backwards to ensure everything was prepared. Usually these shows happened on the weekend. To make that personal sacrifice there had better be a measurable return, so the rep would state a broad sales goal. Then estimate how many customers would need to buy on average and what applications should be highlighted given the clientele. Which products were needed and what accessories and consumables must also be packed. Everything would be cleaned, maintained, and organized so that when executing the plan, cards were stacked in the rep's favor.

To Pitch or Not to Pitch?

Sales professionals use the term *pitch* loosely. In the strictest sense, to pitch is to use a planned speech to persuade someone to buy something.

In today's buying environment, pitching in the strictest sense, seldom works. The customer will raise their defenses, and you will come off as a traditional salesperson. Cookie cutter simply doesn't work.

Selling is like a pick-up game of basketball where there are no rehearsed plays. Draw on good fundamentals to win by adapting to the situation in the moment to yield the desired results. In other words, just have a conversation. If the sales professional is an expert, is cognizant about listening, and has some competence in the aforementioned sales techniques, the sale will move forward.

The Elevator Pitch and Memorable Tag Lines

Sales professionals should always be prepared to concisely and consistently convey what it is the company they represent does. This may seem a bit hypocritical after the anti-pitch advice, but this qualifies as a fundamental that does need to be canned and rehearsed. The last thing a company needs is for sales professionals to go rogue with how they describe the company.

I've worked with companies that allowed reps full liberty in describing what they did, and it was nearly always a stretch on what the company actually did. Think thirty reps, thirty different ways to describe the company, all of them inaccurate.

It's an essential corporate function to provide official talking points about the company to employees for public dissemination. Development, though, can start among the most creative sales reps and receive final approval from marketing and upper management. In the end the tag lines and elevator pitches become part of the corporate identity, and the organization should be dogmatic about using them verbatim.

The elevator pitch is a standard way to describe what the company does. The premise is that the ideal customer you are courting steps into an elevator with you and you have to convey what the company does before the elevator doors open again.

A great team exercise is to spitball ways to describe the company. Then narrow the list down to the top three. Lastly, get approval on the final version from other functions before putting it in use in public. The team can then do a twenty-five-word pitch, break it down to ten words, then to one word.

My personal favorite is the rhyme tag line. This succinct description is memorable and inserts a bit of humor into the conversation with customers, either upon introduction to help break the ice, or upon departure to help the meeting stick. Ultimately, the pitch or tag line that is most comfortable should be used when someone asks, "What do you do?"

As a thought exercise, let's create some pitches and tag lines.

Consider an environmental company that connects green advocates with organizations that tackle climate change. Let's call the fictitious nonprofit *Save Earth Mama*.

Elevator pitch: *The weather has become unpredictable and extreme, as carbon emissions grow, so does weather volatility. Removing carbon from the atmosphere is scientifically proven to attack climate change head on. At Save Earth Mama we connect people interested in doing their part to help save the planet with front line organizations that extract carbon from the atmosphere by expanding coastal ecosystems and planting trees in open spaces worldwide.*

Twenty-five words: *Reducing atmospheric carbon proactively combats climate change. Save Earth Mama connects people with entities that actively expand forests and coastal ecosystems, greatly reducing atmospheric carbon.*

Ten words: *Saving the planet by connecting like-minded individuals to reduce carbon.*

One word: *Planet.*

Rhyme: *At Save Earth Mama, we reduce the planet drama!*

Climate change is no joke, of course, but the takeaway here is sales professionals should be able to succinctly plug their company in a sanctioned consistent manner whenever the opportunity arises.

Over the Phone

So, what about phone skills? They're a hugely important part of the business and often overlooked for focus on in-person techniques. Let's try to remedy that.

The single most important thing to do when speaking on the phone– smile.

Smiling when appropriate is good practice face to face without question, but everyone can gain from smiling more when speaking over the phone. Smiling is the greatest influence on tonality. If you don't believe me, run the following brief experiment with a friend or colleague. Without providing context, ask someone who is notoriously monotone to leave you a voicemail with a simple script you've provided. Then have them do it a second time smiling as genuinely throughout as possible. There will likely be a marked difference between the two messages.

Based on a recommendation from a sales manager, we purchased small mirrors that we placed at each sales rep's desk in the call center to reinforce their training on smiling when speaking over the phone. The mirror prop worked well initially, but once the novelty wore off, reps reverted to their previous selves. Adjusting tactics, we would play recordings of calls we observed of reps when they were smiling for parts of the call, versus when they weren't. With that proof, over time they adopted smiling as part of their normal routine and the more they did it, the more natural and engaging the tone became.

"How do you spell that?" Reps get creative when it comes to confirming spelling over the phone with customers. I've done many a double take when hearing things like, "G as in goat, A as in armadillo . . ." It is unprofessional and confusing to use a uniquely phonetic alphabet.

If you often find yourself working over the phone where exchanging contact information is common, you should know the standard phonetic alphabet. At the very least, there should be a crib sheet for reference at your desk or in your vehicle for field reps. Avoid costly errors and frustration by getting the information down accurately the first time. "Your email is 'A' as in Alpha . . ."

Below find a list of the standard phonetic alphabet.

A – Alpha	J – Juliet	S – Sierra
B – Bravo	K – Kilo	T – Tango
C – Charlie	L – Lima	U – Uniform
D – Delta	M – Mike	V – Victor
E – Echo	N – November	W – Whiskey
F – Foxtrot	O – Oscar	X – X-ray
G – Golf	P – Papa	Y – Yankee
H – Hotel	Q – Quebec	Z – Zulu
I – India	R – Romeo	

Have you ever spoken with someone who causes you to cringe when pronouncing the name of a town or city differently from locals? In sales, mispronouncing the name of a customer's town illustrates that you are an outsider, and that can completely derail rapport building.

I've heard Louisville pronounced Lou-is-vill by outsiders, while locals pronounce it Lou-a-vul. How about Tucson (too-son) incorrectly pronounced Tuck-son? Then there are the truly challenging, such as towns on the Hawaiian Islands. We had a recording of a rep circulate around the company. The rep struggled numerous times to pronounce Kuamalapau (pronounced Kah-OO-ma-LAH-pah-OO) while ending a call with a customer, truly cringe-worthy!

Whether it's Osawatomie (Oh-so-WAH-tah-mee), Kansas, or Coeur d'Alene (kore-duh-LANE), Idaho, there is a simple workaround so that salespeople sound like locals. Simply type into a search engine, "how to pronounce . . .", and voilà (wa-lah), you will have your answer. There are several websites with fairly comprehensive pronunciation resources that should be bookmarked for quick reference. Be informed before the call and have backups for reference so the conversation stays on course.

Selling Is Psychological

It's nice to see that higher education institutions are increasingly offering sales degrees and certifications. You can find sales courses at these institutions under the business department. An argument can be made that sales courses should be under psychology instead. There are different types of buyers, frame of mind greatly determines outcomes, and getting into the customers mind is part of selling. There are entire books devoted to the subject, and I'm not going to purport to be an expert, so I'll just leave it at sales is just as much psychology as it is business.

Along those lines, when you think of a successful salesperson, what type of personality do you think of? If you said extroverts, you have good reason. Extroverts gravitate towards sales positions since they are comfortable socially, generally enthusiastic, and assertive. Extroverts thrive in social environments, where introverts often feel drained because it takes effort.

What if I were to tell you that there is no evidence to prove definitively that extroverts make the best salespeople. In fact, anecdotally I can prove the closer to the extrovert archetype a salesperson is, the more likely they are to be horrible salespeople. No way? Okay, how well do extreme extroverts listen? How likely are prototypical extroverts willing to relinquish the spot at the center of attention? Introverts listen well and prefer to stay out of the limelight. If only we could combine the social traits of extroverts with the listening skills of introverts.

Where personalities fall on the archetypical spectrum greatly determines how effective they can be in sales. Those personalities closer to the middle, where they more naturally use the social traits of extroverts and the listening skills of introverts, are markedly better. The term for these folks is ambiverts, and if you are one or have them in your organization, congratulations[vi]!

When I started off in sales, everyone around was an extrovert. Some customers and fellow reps openly questioned how I was in sales since I was so quiet. I was even accused of being cagy by a coworker, partly because I naturally fall on the introvert spectrum. Of course, when I have something of value to say I channel my inner extrovert! All kidding aside, evidence (scientific and anecdotal) suggest that sales professionals who can strike a balance between extraversion and introversion do much better in the profession.

The Single Most Impactful Activity in Sales

Late in life I discovered what I knew I was missing and what could have made my life in sales a lot easier—networking. *Networking* was a bad word for me. I have to fall on my sword here because I was adamant that networking was disingenuous in some way. The fact is the higher to the executive level your prospects are, or the more affluent, the more necessary it will be to have a warm intro to have a chance at getting their business.

Oddly enough, I step out of my comfort zone and network now when it's arguably less important than when I was a sales rep in charge of my entire pipeline. I've come to discover that networking has too many benefits to ignore. If you are like me and it makes you feel uncomfortable, just try to help where you can with those you connect with. I've done everything from making warm intros, to mentoring, to pro-bono sales diagnostics, all of which was gratifying and demonstrates to me that networking is not evil after all.

Juxtapose networking to a low impact activity like cold calling. Let's take it even a step further, a reliable SDR provided prequalified hot lead gleaned from cold calling. Which connection is more trustworthy for the prospective customer, a warm introduction from a friend/acquaintance, or the stranger on the phone passing the call on to the AE (you)? In a world where we are inundated with messages, warm introductions from a network connection stands out to a far greater extent.

My suggestion: when connecting with someone, be mindful to see if you can link them to someone else or provide something of value. You shouldn't expect anything in return, though there is such a thing as the Law of Reciprocity. In short, if you do something for me, I feel obliged to do something for you. Without expecting much in return it is good practice to pay it forward, you never know when someone in your network will turn out to make a significant difference.

Reciprocity can take the form of material, emotional, or financial means. A way to think of material reciprocity is between neighbors where a tree has fallen and a chainsaw is borrowed or the neighbor cuts up the tree to help clear his neighbor's property of the obstacle. Emotional reciprocity can be a simple compliment. When someone gives you a compliment do you get the urge to counter with a compliment? If so, that's emotional reciprocity. If you help someone save or make a considerable amount of money, do you think they will feel obliged to return the favor somehow? Folks like these we call active references because they will go above and beyond a warm intro, you are their hero! A satisfied customer can be a great source in your network for warm intros and referrals. In the end, reciprocity is an urge to do something in return, so do something nice as you network, and it may pay dividends.

A word of caution, though: reciprocity is a double-edged sword. Part of the reason I was opposed to networking for the better part of my life was because it forced me to interact with people I was not genuinely interested in or didn't think I would like for many reasons. In hindsight, when I was introduced to many people that fell into this category, I acted aloof. Some proved to be jerks as suspected. Most were harmless, so I'll never know. Many more than those who were jerks turned out to be ok, they actually were of value either at a personal level or professionally much to my surprise. I have to say, I squandered countless opportunities because I prejudged. In some instances, if someone I just met rubbed me the wrong way, I was very direct, which shocked people. Here comes the other edge of the reciprocity sword. If you do something hurtful to someone else, they will want to get even, they will want to do something hurtful back to you. Bottom line, be nice and just walk away, otherwise you are only hurting yourself by burning bridges.

The irony here is that I've gone from anti-networker to super connector (relative to my capabilities). Not only do I match good sales professionals with job opportunities where they are a fit without them asking, I reach out to parents associated in some way to my kid's extracurricular activities. With my closest friends far away and spread out all over the place, it's nice to be able to get to know new people, develop friendships, and share experiences with each other. It is interesting to discover what people do and learn their personal stories. I'm clearly a networking late bloomer! If you're in the same boat, rest assured there's still time to learn how to network too.

CHAPTER 6

Today's Buying Environment

Having taken a deep dive into the seller's world—focusing on tactics and techniques—let's shift to the other side of the sales equation: buying. To truly understand how best to sell to customers, it's critically important to go through the buyer's journey.

Understanding what a buyer goes through establishes an appreciation that informs the sales professional on how best to serve the customer. The first modules during the onboarding process of sales professionals should include experiencing the buyer's journey. In fact, I encourage other non-sales functions to also go through the typical buyer's journey at their organizations to better understand the business. Whether in tech building "product" on the platform, or part of product R & D in a more traditional sense, the buyer's journey is invaluable to gaining customer orientation.

Let's take a step back for a moment. Before the customer actually goes through the buying experience at your company, that customer has to get there first. Based on research conducted by CEB (now Gartner) the average B2B purchase decision is already 57 percent complete and over ten information sources are used prior to supplier engagement.

While those numbers vary by sales complexity, they generally mean sales professionals can barely influence the purchase decision because suppliers are contacted so late in the buying process that sales professionals are just used for fulfillment[vii]. In short, the supplier that offers the most for the least wins, regardless of fit.

Many sales professionals (me included) would argue that the customer may be doing themselves a disservice because they may be selecting a completely wrong product or service for their application influenced through confirmation bias, misinformation, or influence from novices in the field. When customers are already more than halfway to making a purchase, it is next to impossible to change their minds.

There is hope! If marketing has done its job, the initial stages where the customer is learning can be influenced by company-driven insights. Through a combination of influencers, articles, customer blogs, and traditional marketing collateral, the customer has a greater chance to make an informed decision. If solid, insightful information exists for the customer and the marketing department has done the job, it stacks the cards in the sales professional's favor, particularly if it encourages the customer to speak with a salesperson before going further down the buying path.

I've often had customers want a product for a specific application, mostly because they were replacing the old product they used with the latest and greatest without considering a different process for the application. They come prepared, having read online materials, narrowed the field down to the top three picks, and are about to pull the trigger after seeing the product in action or speaking with someone at the company in order to confirm their decision.

I had a B2C customer who was insistent that he needed a certain expensive replacement product for his application, which he perceived would make him more productive by a few percentage points. I carefully asked how he came to that conclusion (never use the word "why" as it puts people on the defensive). I then told him there may be a product in a different category he may want to consider instead, only because it would make the process twice as fast, eliminate the need for an extra employee, and could be used for more applications that fall within his wheelhouse. Now that I had his attention, I demonstrated this product in a mock version of his application, again underscoring with facts how working smarter would make him more profitable while standing out from the competition. I waited silently as he contemplated his next move. My product was more expensive, and I was asking him to deviate from a process he was comfortable with. Like so many others, he fully bought in, becoming a repeat customer (and brand advocate) for many years.

Here's another example, this time B2B. Years ago I was trying to land a potentially large prospective account that did high volume with competitive brands in our category. It was a third-generation business, so they were an established and successful organization, but set in their ways. They were the go-to source for customers in their area, and as a business without much competition locally, they were complacent. They brought up a product that sold from competitors simply by sitting back and taking orders all day. Through a series of leading questions, I discovered what their gross margins were, how much handling that product cost them, and average amount of returns. They also were sure to remind me that the competitor's product was a third of the price of ours. After confirming the information, they provided about the competitor's product, I created a table on a piece of paper and went through the numbers together until we came to a net profit number. Then I created another column with our product. The look in their eyes said it all as it turned out that they would have to sell six times the product to achieve the same profit. We agreed there were also sunk costs because of the high amount of processed returns versus what our low return rate was historically. The icing on the cake was that I had proof that in part because our products were designed as a system north of 75 percent of customers came back within a year to make multiple purchases of our brand's products. I finished with a bit of tactful emotional appeal by stating that savvy businesses bring in our products because they are more profitable, draw quality repeat customers, and generally help elevate the business. Ok, I did bundle logical insights with emotional appeal (when I appealed to their pride), sales professionals should know to do what neuroscience has proven; people need logic and emotion to buy[viii]. I walked out with an opening order.

Sales Funnel

Earlier we mentioned the sales funnel when talking about the sales pipeline. Now it's time to circle back and take a deeper look at the funnel, which relates directly to a buyer's experience. The below graphic shows a typical sales funnel.

The buying process correlates with the buyer's journey and the sales funnel. While the customer purchase experience has four high level stages (learn, clarify needs, evaluate options, purchase decision), the sales funnel has six stages; awareness, discovery, evaluation, intent, purchase, loyalty.

Let's examine both the purchase experience and the sales funnel in greater detail.

The customer purchase experience begins with learning. This takes the form of learning about the next generation replacement of an existing product or service, options on the market along with competitors that may address the application, and what is trending for the application. This first stage is heavily marketing driven. In some instances, learning also means assessing current approaches.

The second stage brings clarity to the first by identifying needs from "nice to haves" to "must haves." The features with the most closely aligned benefits to address the application take priority here. In short, the customer is searching for solutions.

Reaching the customer in these first two stages when they can best be influenced is the sweet spot for sales professionals. To be clear, I'm being honest, not pushing for manipulation at these stages. Sales professionals need to sell the customer based on product fit and not just to earn a sale which will come back to burn them in the form of a return, bad review, or both if it isn't in the best interests of the customer.

Zeroed in on the type of product, the customer then lists suppliers of competitive products to consider in the third stage of evaluating options. Brand name recognition plays a role depending on the type of product, supplier capability, and options that reduce the risk of a bad purchase. Sales professionals can still intervene here, though it will take some backtracking to get the customer to the previous stage.

In the last stage, the supplier who offers more features for a lower price is prioritized. This is the equivalent of selecting an *RFP* (request for proposal) where the supplier with the best terms, pricing, and the one offering the most features gets selected for the purchase. While there is still hope at stage III to earn the sale, once the customer is at stage IV the buying decision is already made. It will take an act of god to convince the customer to reconsider.

Putting it all together, we see the sales funnel is the buyer's first contact with your company, all the way through purchase. Sales funnels are wide at the top and narrow on the bottom. Sales funnels help sales professionals because they assist them in delivering the appropriate message at the right time to customers, improving the customer journey. A clearly defined sales funnel also helps sales professionals' companies by more accurately forecasting sales and how to scale their sales process.

At the top of funnel, the customer is researching and learning about the problem they need solved. Found at the very top of the funnel are customers who haven't even identified the problem; they just have symptoms and are trying to identify the problem in order to solve it. The customer is in stage I, learning. They want to feel confident before speaking with anyone on the topic. This is where customers transition into leads, organically or through marketing efforts.

The funnel is wide here for a reason. Most leads won't qualify. For those that do, the sales professional is engaged in discovery, where qualified customers have their needs identified and confirmed. For the customer, they are likely in the second stage of the customer purchasing experience, where the sales professional's company may be one of several vendors being considered.

As the sales professional moves lower down the funnel, we find the customer moving to evaluation. Here, given the information provided and the right product fit, the sales professional makes an offer that solves the customer's problem. This dovetails into the intent stage, where the customer will negotiate, accept, or reject the offer. When the offer is accepted and the customer makes a purchase, the deal is finally closed in the eyes of the sales professional.

While the customer purchase experience is over, unless the sale is strictly transactional, the sales funnel contains one more critical stage—loyalty. As mentioned in chapter two, customer retention is an important component that not only improves the health of the organization but leads to recurring business for sales professionals. There are a host of other benefits to help the business quantify *customer lifetime value* (CLV).

$$\text{CLV} = \sum_{t=1}^{T} \left(\frac{C_t}{(1+d)^t} r^{t-1} \right) - A$$

A = Acquisition cost
C = Cash flow
d = Discount rate
t = Time period
r = Retention rate

The above formula is provided for analytical types and as a scientific basis of proof that a predictable value can be assigned to customer loyalty.

CLV helps quantify how well you identify with customers, how much customers appreciate your products/services, and where to improve. CLV also provides a predictable number to forecast revenue of existing customers, which can be used in funding rounds or in the case of a liquidation event. From a YoY sales and marketing standpoint, it helps inform how budget will be allocated for marketing spend, how sales goals will be structured, and even what type of salesperson will be required to support strategic intent. Depending on the volume, how large CLV may be, and economic conditions, corporate strategy may adapt to focus more (or less) on customer retention over new customer acquisition. Personnel in the form of organization and support are greatly affected by these decisions.

A Note on Marketing

Since we have ventured into the realm of marketing, I'm compelled to go through the marketing analysis model as it also helps provide a more comprehensive understanding of the customer, organization and the competitive landscape.

A version of the model looks like this:

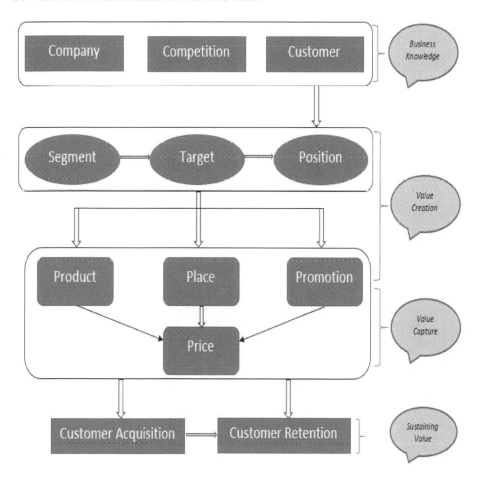

During the first day of new sales rep orientation as VP of Sales at a tech startup, I would go through the marketing analysis model with new hires even though we didn't have a marketing department per se. Doing this interactively certainly resonated. The new reps would attempt to tell me who the three Cs were. After that brief discussion, they would understand the business more. Then we would dive into industry segment, target, and our position (STPs), followed by defining the three Ps, with the understanding that all of this created customer value. Price is how we captured value, and customers were how we sustained value. Although academic and highly structured, it seemed to be a good exercise since it made high level concepts a lot more tangible for everyone.

Recognizing Customer Types

To increase the chances of success for all reps, the organization should have clearly defined customer personas. These are profiles that categorize the ideal customer based on market research and existing customer data. Knowing desired behaviors of target customers such as how they learn, plan, try/buy, use, and advocate, enables the entire sales organization to have greater success with their selling efforts.

The customer persona should include demographic information, mindset and motivation, category attitude, and resources used in the buying process. Organizations that are serious about scaling sales need to have data driven customer personas fully developed to support their sales staff. Leaving it to the sales rep to come up with customer personas is a fool's errand. Though it can be done depending on the level of sale complexity, it is not scalable or repeatable.

Another way to better understand customers is by recognizing where they fall on the innovation adoption curve. Originally applied in 1957 to agriculture and home economics, the metric was later applied to innovation in the book, *Diffusion of Innovations* by Everett Rogers[ix]. The curve highlights five sections of social buying behavior.

Adoption/Innovation Curve

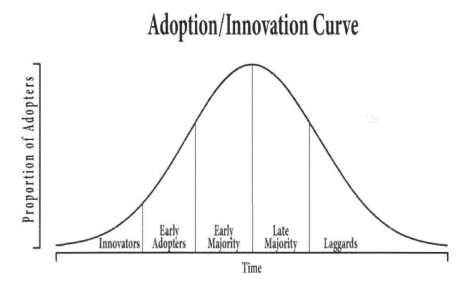

Here is a breakdown of each section:

Innovators (2.5 percent of population) – on the fringe, they experiment with cutting edge products and lifestyles. Folks in this section are found to be prosperous and highly educated.

As a sales professional, these are your new product beta testers. They will assist you with product refinements and possibly provide some advice on who to target.

Early Adopters (13.5 percent of population) – also highly educated, they are progressive, less experimental, and more informed decision minded. They embrace change when it makes sense. They have influence in their communities, pushing the innovation out to the broader culture.

For sales professionals, early adopters can be product advocates that will help create critical mass to cross the chasm into the mainstream.

Early Majority (34 percent of population) – also socially active and influential in their communities, they don't seek out change. Rather they accept it as it becomes more ubiquitous.

Sales professionals selling to early majority customers are engaged with a type of customer who weighs the benefits of innovation with costs.

Late Majority (34 percent of population) – reluctant to accept change, skeptical, and usually hold out until they are forced to adopt innovations.

Sales professionals pitching to late majority customers should be mindful to convey change as least disruptive as possible. Keeping it simple, proving through demonstration that the innovation is easily adaptable, may yield better results. The value proposition should be locked-in and testimonials should be accessible to assist with closing the sale.

Laggards (16 percent of population)—they do not accept change unless forced upon them. Reliability and low cost are their main drivers, they are uncomfortable with change.

This group is being forced to change because a product may be obsolete or will be discontinued. Sales professionals should be careful not to try to upsell, get too technical, or boast of the new product. This group of customers will only become more exacerbated under those conditions. Walking the customer through the basics of use is a helpful approach.

There were situations when I was a sales rep where I could have benefited with the knowledge of the innovation adoption curve and the marketing analysis model, both of which I learned later when I went back to school to earn my MBA in order to be a better sales leader.

It did help me though in that role. The first time was in discussions with our VP of Marketing, when I called him out on some unorthodox strategies that contradicted the marketing analysis model. He was creative and had good intuition, but he had a tendency to do things without proper preparation, which we in sales felt downstream all the time. When I called him out on something fairly significant, I referenced the marketing framework, which he dismissed completely. He laughed it off, but I didn't. Plans were restructured and formalized. Disaster was averted.

Sales Versus Marketing

"Marketing is just sales with a degree to back it up!"

Statements like that are first shots across the bow and fighting words between departments. Strangely, there tends to be an adversarial relationship between sales and marketing departments[x]. Much of it starts at the leadership level for each, where communication breaks down and competition between sales reps and folks in the marketing department incites degenerative behavior.

World class sales organizations, however, build bridges instead of walls between the sales and marketing departments. When sales and marketing are working in concert, magical things happen, and growth seems to be turbocharged. Though completely anecdotal, in my experience when there is a VP of Sales and Marketing or someone in charge of both departments (other than the CEO), smoother collaboration happens.

Recognizing the differences between sales and marketing creates appreciation for the value each brings. Philosophically, marketing takes a broad customer view, casting a wider net. Sales takes a narrower view of customer needs. Marketing thinks in terms of share of wallet; they are market-share oriented. Sales is volume oriented.

Marketing focuses on customer groups. Sales groups customers and focuses on individuals. Both marketing and sales add value individually, but together they are a force to be reckoned with.

Marketing's superpower is the process of researching and then producing, which can steer salespeople in the right ways to have the most impact on their efforts. Salespeople expect marketing to provide carpet bombing through ads, brand name recognition, and thought-leadership content in order for sales to storm the beaches to victory.

When sales and marketing work well together, sales provides market intelligence to inform strategy, and marketing provides sales with quantified direction to leverage their offerings. Sales efforts are closely coordinated with marketing initiatives; both teams are supporting each other running successful campaigns.

Lastly, consider sales and marketing as a marriage. Like any good marriage, a fair amount of attention, respect, tolerance, and communication are required to ensure the relationship stays healthy. Sales leaders need to run point on keeping that marriage together and keeping it strong—no divorces on your watch!

CHAPTER 7

Transitioning to Sales Leadership

The Promotion Dilemma

Time and again, organizations promote their top salespeople to sales-leadership roles. As is often the case, the superstar sales rep becomes a mediocre sales manager, resulting in a wash or net negative ROI for the company. I'm guilty of it myself: rewarding hardworking reps that consistently performed only to find out that I did them and the company a disservice by promoting them. Those responsible for advocating on behalf of the newly promoted sales manager tend to spend an inordinate amount of time developing, supporting, and intervening to provide proof that the right decision to promote was made and to get the sales manager on the right path. In many instances, that support doesn't even exist because the assumption is the superstar rep should by default be a superstar manager by passing on the best practices that worked in the previous role and creating multipliers with direct reports. That approach sets up the employee for failure and is irresponsible.

However, there's a better way to promote sales reps to managers, increasing the chances that the decision was the right decision, and one that will pay dividends down the road. Just because a rep is crushing goals, doesn't mean they are slated for promotion to manager. Think about it: does it make sense to take your top producing rep out of the field?

Instead, the price for admission into management should be consistent sales performance, where the rep meets or exceeds goals for a minimum amount of time that accounts for anomalies like seasonality. The next criteria should be reps who follow process, and, after implementing for a reasonable period, offer actionable improvement recommendations. That cohort of reps can be further screened to have positive mental attitudes, leadership capabilities as demonstrated when they are in groups during sales meetings, supportive tendencies towards coworkers, and to be people who follow company marching orders as well as sincerely believe in the mission. Generally, these characteristics, *alongside* the hard-working proof of sales performance, add up to the best management candidates.

That Big Promotion Means Big Relationship Changes

Sales reps who get promoted have reason to celebrate. They should also take a deep breath and be aware that their lives are going to change in ways they can't anticipate. Those deeply personal discussions, those friendships—they end the moment your promotion announcement is made.

This very thing happened to me, and it was bizarre at first. People I had considered friends were suddenly not as close to me. Moreover, they were careful about what they shared with me. It's important not to take the shift personally. Make no mistake, this change in behavior doesn't come out of envy, but rather out of fear, as reps don't want to jeopardize their jobs by oversharing. In the long run it's probably for the best anyways. Consider that the new sales manager needs to hold former friends accountable when they don't meet standards. They also need to hold certain things closer to the vest than before from a variety of professional and organizational reasons.

When I was about to promote sales reps to manager, I would advise that they create a file to contain all the notes of praise they would receive. Most of those messages are sincere. Some are motivated by job security. Regardless, they are likely well-earned, and keeping them for reference is definitely helpful. When a particular direct report is driving you crazy, reviewing the congratulatory note that rep sent may take the sting out of the situation. They will help when you feel like you're failing, and during the most challenging times you will feel that way. Reading those words of praise will lift your spirits and come in handy when those who gave you praise should receive praise because they are taking turns climbing the corporate ladder.

Some companies onboard sales leaders better than others. With that in mind, the newly promoted rep should be sure blind spots are being addressed so they can reach their full potential in the new role.

For example, if a rep isn't proficient at Excel, they should be enrolled in a progression of classes paid for by the company to gain the required proficiency. If they need to be more technically savvy with the products, they should have additional onboarding with a focus on spending time with technical experts. If the person driving the promotion cannot identify the skill gaps and propose a curriculum to address those, the newly promoted manager should speak up. By remaining silent, the new manager is putting the team at risk and potentially jeopardizing their boss's job.

I've found it works best when the new manager has a candid discussion with the direct supervisor to gain a complete understanding of the new role, what the day to day looks like, land mines to avoid, and goals that need to be achieved. After reflecting on that, the new manager should bring up skill gaps that require company investment, supported with already researched options (e.g. secondary education courses) that the supervisor can then get approved without delay. The thing to remember: Everyone has gaps. The newly promoted manager has the advantage of a clean track record, aiding potential decision makers in more clearly seeing that is the time to get the support required to be successful.

When I was a sales rep and our company was growing exponentially, we brought on a rep to cover some of my states, splitting the territory to be able to manage it effectively. This rep came with more corporate experience than all of us. He was an extremely Type A personality, and he claimed he could do a lot of things.

Personally, my BS meter was going off, but when a rep with so much experience comes along and is highly recommended by credible people in the industry, the decision is heavily influenced towards making the hire. When the President of the subsidiary asked me what I thought, I recall saying, "If he does half the things he says he can, you'll have your best rep hire."

Ultimately, we hired Cory. He proved to be even more passionate than we anticipated, about everything! Sales meetings were spirited, thanks to Cory. Goals were never enough, with Cory challenging everyone to push for more aggressive gains. He was very competitive; he constantly threw down the gauntlet. I kind of liked it, to be honest. I tried to learn from his ability to bond with people quickly, to speak with authority, and to seemingly know everything. I gave him the benefit of the doubt; after all, he was my senior and a tenured rep from a well-respected company.

After a year or so, the President of our company in the U.S. requested that I ride with Cory in his territory. I was given no further information. We weren't monitoring leaderboards at the time, but I knew I was the only rep in the company who hit goals the previous year. I didn't know Cory was struggling. I also didn't know he was paid nearly twice as much as me, or that he was producing significantly less than half of my numbers. It was probably best I didn't know any of that. It let me go in blind with the best of intentions.

We were to spend the week together, working the mountain states. About a day and a half into it, Cory had a personal issue with his wife, so he had to cancel his trip and get home. I continued to work his accounts since appointments were already made and I had nothing else set for my territory. In addition, my travel expenses couldn't be recovered (still commission rep minded). I made the best of it, resolved some issues, took some orders, and along the way travelled in a beautiful part of the country during the right time of year.

Cory called on me for other help, and I gladly obliged. We spent some more time together later that year, discussing where the company was going and what ambitions we had. He volunteered that he needed to be national accounts manager, that the position he was in was just temporary. He also proclaimed to me that if I was ever promoted to western region sales manager, "I will work my ass off for you." I was genuinely appreciative of that promise.

Then it came. I was promoted, and Cory was one of five other direct reports I inherited. Within minutes of the announcement, I received a call from Cory that went to voicemail because I was in a spotty area. About 30 minutes later, when I had reception, I listened to it. I was shocked. Cory was not ready to do everything he could for me. Cory was *pissed*, and he let me know how undeserving I was of the promotion, how he was the best qualified person, and how I was all these nasty things I'd never considered of anyone in the company, much less myself. For a good part of the day, I was shell shocked.

A steady stream of messages praising my promotion came from others. At the end of the day, my boss, the U.S. subsidiary president, called to congratulate me. The first thing he asked was if Cory had called me. I asked if there was a reason for that question? He said Cory called him shortly after the announcement went out. He had nothing but praise and positive things to say about me, and how it was the right decision that the company would benefit from for a long time. I actually thought he was joking. In hindsight, it may have been the opposite—a similar rant that was left on my voicemail—but my boss was magnanimous in many ways, and if spinning the call he had with Cory to get me on the right foot was what needed to be done, then I was going to accept what he told me as gospel.

Right away, I had to deal with what became my first prima donna. There was a major conflict with a top account in Cory's territory. The clash of personalities exacerbated what was probably a solvable business problem. When I arrived, the owner was literally throwing our products out into the snow. I had to get between the two of them before they got into a brawl. They were screaming at each other without regard for the customers around them. For the first time I was glad that Cory made the unnecessary and unapproved vehicle purchase of a raised full bed truck. Luckily it was less than an hour from his home, so we made a couple of trips, packed all the inventory, and had it prepped the next day for shipping back to our facility. I terminated that channel partner relationship and denied reinstatement.

As we've discussed and seen, transitioning from a rep to a sales leader poses a significant shift in relationships. I was anticipating an even greater relationship shift when a couple years later I was slated for another promotion. The official company announcement was supposed to go out at the beginning of the year. And although I was already taking on many of the new role's responsibilities, there was no official announcement until the first day in April. I was at a stop light in my car when I saw an email notification come over from our company President with the subject line, "New VP of Sales." I quickly pulled over and read, in disbelief, several paragraphs about . . . Cory, his accomplishments, and why he was the best choice for the role.

Then it dawned on me. It was April 1. I called the company President, and after a bit of probing, he was extremely satisfied that he fooled me. I was satisfied that he would send out the official announcement of my promotion first thing the next day.

Of course, I warned my boss that there would be payback for the practical joke. One-year later when he arrived at his office, he found an email sent from me in his inbox marked with high priority. The subject line read, "Letter of Resignation." In the body of the email I stated that, "the attachment says it all." When opening the attachment, it said in large, bold font, "April Fool's!" He called me after opening it, and when I answered, he said, "That was a good one! I'm not messing with you again."

If you're the right person for the promotion, be prepared for everything to change and to have the tenacity to adopt a fun attitude towards challenging situations. Coworkers that are considered friends will do an about face on your relationship and on promises made, as evidenced by Cory. When it is your turn to slate someone for a promotion, there is a right way and a wrong way to determine promotions in sales, hard work alone is just the first of many criteria. The newly promoted owe it to coworkers to fill skill gaps for the new role, and never forget where they came from because it will ground them with the necessary respect for team members. Along the way you will build memories together and feel rewarded for helping others reach their full potential.

CHAPTER 8

Sales Leadership

Note the use of sales leader instead of sales manager in this chapter's title. Some people look at the two words and wonder is there really a difference. As we started to unpack last chapter: *yes*. Language is always full of nuance. So, let's dig deeper into the difference between leaders and managers before more fully unpacking what leadership means in sales.

Managers do things right, executing on marching orders and following the playbook. Leaders do the right things, fostering a team culture built on integrity. Managers get things done through delegation. Leaders get things done through trust and motivation. Managers lead by authority—they have subordinates. Leaders lead by inspiration—they have followers. Inventory and process (things) should be managed. People should be led!

When a sales rep is promoted to a sales leader, the real work begins. Sales leaders who are good at their jobs recognize they have an awesome responsibility because they have a direct impact on the livelihood of their team members. Previously, as a sales rep, if they didn't move the sale forward, there was another opportunity to pursue. That simply isn't the case in a sales leadership role! If the sales leader cannot sell the team member on goals or efficacy of products or services, then credibility is lost. People's livelihoods suffer. Relationships suffer.

Furthermore, the sales leader must get buy-in from the entire sales organization, which is pivotal to achieving the company's goals. The higher the climb up the career ladder, the greater magnitude of responsibility for the sales leader. One way to think of it: the more you climb on your career journey, accruing more responsibilities and promotions, the more you have to lose.

Establishing Credibility with the New Sales Team

The initial transition period is a golden opportunity for newly promoted sales leaders to set the tone for a constructive team relationship. So much rides on that first one-on-one meeting between newly promoted sales leaders and team members. Based on the venting I've heard from reps across sales organizations in a variety of industries, promoted sales leaders lacking credibility is a common theme. Team members aren't sold on their new sales leaders. As a result, the newly promoted sales leader starts off working from a position of weakness. A plethora of evidence supports that good employees leave companies because they have bad bosses[xi]. If a new sales leader can't even get out of the starting blocks with direct reports because they haven't effectively sold themselves, the relationship is doomed.

Recently I was speaking with a friend and top-performing sales rep I respect. He expressed his frustration about management changes to his organization and how he had a vote of no confidence for his latest direct supervisor. After several leadership changes, none of which had stuck, his frustrations seemed understandable and not isolated.

Upon their initial meeting, his new boss introduced himself and went into performance goals as well as required changes to administrative activities "for all reps that worked <u>for</u> [him]." This immediately created stress risers in the foundation of their relationship.

My friend went for the jugular, "How long have you been with the company?" he asked.

The newly promoted manager was caught flat-footed, responding that he'd been with the company for about two years (my friend was on his sixteenth year). Then he tried to defend his position by explaining he had other experience in another industry with a different company. It probably didn't help that my friend was almost old enough to be his dad.

"After only two years, there is no way you can possibly understand the products and our customers," my friend responded. His new boss didn't have much of a retort.

My friend was visibly upset while conveying the story. He expressed how he was losing sleep over working with his new boss and provided some more examples of how his boss was throwing out objectives that they were top-down mandates, the polar opposite of the way to approach a top-performing tenured sales rep who had been crushing it for years. He was considering making a career change.

"What if he introduced himself, referenced a few of your top accomplishments, and then acknowledged that he could never know as much about the products as you given your experience, would that have made a difference?" I asked.

"Hell yes!"

"If he then laid out that his sole purpose was to help you be efficient and focused in order for you to be more successful without having to work so hard, would you be open to working with him?" I went on.

"Of course!"

"Then he went into the performance goals for the year and how you two could work together to accomplish those goals, supported with concrete examples of his capabilities. Would he have credibility?"

"Steve," my friend said, "I'd follow him anywhere and advocate for him with my coworkers because we all talk. But you're living in an alternate reality. These new managers all do the same thing and in the end the reps share more stories about how horrible our boss is than victories in the field that we can learn from."

It cannot be stressed enough: that transition period is the courting period, and sales leaders need to make their best effort to sell themselves to their team members during this window.

Sales leaders who take the approach that *reps work with them and not for them* help to build that solid relationship foundation. Furthermore, providing acknowledgments and recognizing rep skills demonstrates respect, which is a two-way street. Finally, coming prepared with examples of how the sales leader can support the sales rep from their first meeting underscores the credibility of the relationship.

Curbing Team Negativity

According to the U.S. Bureau of Labor Statistics, the harmful effects of negativity in the workplace costs businesses $3 billion a year. The guiding principle to mitigate the harmful effects of negativity is to make positivity the core of your team's, department's, and company's culture.

That means catching people doing things right rather than drilling them on things they are doing wrong. It means celebrating staff members who serve as examples, without playing favorites. It means inclusion of all and isolation of none. It means treating the symptoms in conflict resolution and discouraging personal attacks. It means providing a safe way for staff to offer feedback for improvement and acting on that feedback. In sales roles such as call centers, where there may be a disproportionate amount of disparaging and negative conversations from customers, it means having a channel to dispose of abusive communications.

At a call center we were transforming, we received some brutally negative communications from customers, and over time it was easy for reps to be impacted. A tactic we used to tackle the negativity was to create a wall of shame where some of the most egregious comments were featured and highlighted. It proved to be cathartic for the reps and something we all laughed about occasionally as we selectively read examples of how people lose control.

We reminded reps that the person who stays in control wins, and those making disparaging comments are the real losers. More than just a coping mechanism, it bonded the team. We balanced that wall of shame with a wall of fame directly across from it. The wall of fame celebrated customer praise for reps, sales victories, and major sales milestones. The wall of fame was significantly more colorful, full, and complete than the wall of shame.

What Great Sales Leaders Look Like

How are great sales leaders identified?

- ✔ Great sales leaders have expertise.
- ✔ Great sales leaders know their craft so well that direct reports take notes as soon as their leader starts talking.
- ✔ Great sales leaders can sell the vision, or where the team needs to go. And they can sell how to get there step by step, making the ambitious believable, and wielding infectious passion.

✔ Great sales leaders know their staff. They are benevolent, yet maintain a high level of accountability, and everyone knows where they stand.

✔ Great sales leaders encourage purpose and develop people to reach their full potential.

✔ Great sales leaders retain talent and attract talent because they are trustworthy and keep the team motivated. World class sales organizations have great sales leaders, where the mantra is, "we are part of something much bigger than ourselves."

Great Sales Leaders are Respectful of Time

Team members dedicated to their sales leader will make personal sacrifices and go the extra mile. They trust and respect their sales leader because the sales leader also trusts and respects them. It's the little things that a sales leader does that shows through action this trust and respect.

When team members are taking personal time (after hours, vacation, etc.), sales leaders must respect boundaries. Sales leaders will hold team members accountable to deadlines, so the sales leader must show by example that commitments are delivered as promised. The simplest thing a sales leader can do to encourage trust and respect, is to start on time and to end on time. Being punctual for every meeting, every call, every conversation, is a simple objective that yields great results.

Early on as a sales leader, the field reps on my team wanted more frequent check-ins that were sensitive to their travel and time constraints. Spread hundreds and even thousands of miles between each other, we agreed on having a weekly huddle via conference call every Tuesday morning at 8 a.m. PST. No more than three items would be on the agenda, and every week a different team member would kick it off. We started on time, and we were done by 8:15, leaving the team updated and armed with the latest info to tackle the week.

The company President learned of these huddles and requested that my counterpart on the other coast implement the same. After mentoring him, he was cut loose to conduct his own huddles with his team. Unfortunately, over the years, his team had accepted tardiness as status quo because their boss was never on time. He was usually last to arrive and went over time. When it came time to implement the weekly huddle, try as he may, he had reps show up to the weekly huddles more than halfway through, while others chose not to show up at all! Worse yet, my counterpart would consistently go over time by thirty to forty-five minutes. Reps checked out during these calls because they were being told rather than being involved.

Aside from the inverse of trust and respect, sales professionals that are habitually late cost the company money! As a cathartic exercise I calculated the amount of time wasted through tardiness alone with this group of sales professionals, assigned an hourly rate based on everyone's pay, and multiplied that by the total amount of time wasted over the course of a year. Incredibly, that team could have hired an additional sales rep with all the costs they wasted around time.

Let me take this a bit deeper when it comes to meetings in general.

Meetings should be structured with clear agendas and intent. If thirty minutes are allocated, but everything can be covered in ten minutes, then give everyone back those twenty minutes. That unexpected gift demonstrates the respect you have for others.

Sadly, that's not usually how meetings go. Instead, there's a tendency to fill every minute, create new topics that force additional meetings, and create more unnecessary work. When done right, meetings produce results, demonstrate respect, and finish on time. When done wrong, meetings beget more meetings, and the participants walk away overwhelmed.

I saw the time waste meetings can become first-hand working at my first tech company. Never in my life had I been pulled into so many different meetings so frequently. That's not to say some of these meetings weren't valuable and necessary. However, most went around in circles and led to more meetings. My preference was to stay out of our HQ in San Francisco so I could get more done. That is until my coworkers filled my calendar with meetings I had to conference into. Then there was no escape. The good news was my sales team (in another location) was starved for productive meetings. So, when I was given the reigns and ran my first meeting (over video conference), I covered everything in seven minutes with twenty-three minutes to spare. By design I was prepared, succinct, and deliberate. Upon informing the team they were getting time back, there was laughter and a team member said, "Best meeting ever, that's how it should be!"

Great Sales Leaders Use Honesty to Inspire

Transparency is a hallmark of great sales leaders, particularly as it relates and directly impacts salespeople. Letting members on the team know where they stand generates trust and respect.

As an executive at a Fortune 500 consumer product group company, Andy had been personally involved with the implementation of two headcount reductions. The decision to let staff go to ensure share-holder value didn't sit well with Andy. It also impacted the company culture and employee morale.

Andy and I discussed how he decided to meet with his team members and lay it all out. He knew he owed it to them to be honest. Nothing would lead to complacency and attrition of some of his best people.

"I told them . . . the company has no loyalty to you!" he said to me. "The days when companies expected employees to stay loyal and in return companies would remain loyal to employees is a thing of the past. Don't work hard for the company. Don't learn new skills or work together to get better for the company. Do it for yourself! Do it for your next job and for your own career development."

The result: employees were motivated in the short and medium term to do their best. They respected Andy's honesty and stayed loyal to him. When they reached a point in their career where they had something better lined up, they took the opportunity.

The Biggest Mistake Sales Leaders Make

Let's run through a few common mistakes sales leaders make.

1. Spending the majority of time planning a plan or approach, rather than committing sufficient time to the inner workings of executing. Plans need to have assigned roles and goals, for instance. Avoid this common mistake by getting down to the nuts and bolts, instead of getting lost in the initial conceptual stages.

2. Spending a disproportionate amount of time in the office, rather than in the field with customers and sales staff. It's in the field where the sales leader can gain proper orientation to the needs of sales staff and customers. Everyone in the sales force should be in lockstep, regardless of headcount, but when strategic intent is not communicated down to the individual, your best assets go in different directions.

3. Failing to communicate effectively, and thereby failing to account for the impact feedback has on the sales staff and on the culture.

The bigger the organization, the more important communication becomes (although it's arguably as important in smaller organizations, or skunk works teams where agility is paramount in order to be able to make the necessary pivots).

Tools exist to assist sales leaders to methodically communicate effectively. The framework I prefer is the 7 Cs of communication: clear, complete, concise, concrete, considerate, correct, and courteous. I'd supplement the 7Cs with an "E"—empathy.

Just as top-performing sales reps have the uncanny ability to empathize enough with customers to be prescriptive with their pitch so it comes off as a perfect fit for the customer's needs, a sales leader should be able to do the same with sales staff. Lack of empathy is the biggest mistake sales leaders make.

To be clear, a measured approach to empathy is required. Just as we don't want the sales rep to give away the store to help a customer out, we also don't want the sales leader to over empathize with staff, which could have consequential effects that may be detrimental to the business.

The beauty: if there are sales leaders already in place, chances are they possess the empathy skills required since they were likely promoted because they proved themselves first as successful sales reps. For various reasons, sales leaders forget about this key component when they get into higher positions. More than ever, they should channel the empathy they used to reach their new position and be mindful to keep it in practice.

Sales leaders should be communicative and use empathy with direct reports. They should get to know their people well—not just their strengths and areas for improvement, but also their preferred communications style and way of learning.

Sales leaders should be prescriptive with their individual team members whenever possible, so the tailored message has the greatest chance to resonate. Of course, when being agile or in large organizations with large teams, this approach may be unrealistic. In such cases, a high-level measure of empathy can work well. Start by never asking sales staff to do anything you wouldn't do yourself.

All of this brings us to delivering feedback, the final consideration to clear communication and empathy. Feedback *must* be delivered in a manner that preserves an individual's dignity. Holding people in the same roles accountable to the same Key Performance Indicators (KPIs) is table stakes. Delivering feedback to encourage better performance is really critical. The sales leader should prepare the discussion carefully, see it from the team member's standpoint, and employ the 7 Cs. As performance reviews come up, sales leaders have a tendency to zero in on what direct reports are doing *wrong*. Instead they should actually be focused on building upon what is being done *right*.

This right-wrong dilemma is a malady of upper management I've seen again and again over the years. It's time to turn those cringe-worthy performance reviews into performance appraisals.

During feedback, bringing up what is being done right and providing concrete examples honors the team member's efforts and keeps motivation high. For influencing improvements, use of transition statements such as: "the area that would make you even more successful at your job," or "I encourage you to hone the skill of," supported with examples showing how outcomes would have been dramatically better in situations where the supported action was better used.

Sales professionals are a truly powerful force when they can be harnessed properly using effective communication and empathy.

Emotional Intelligence (EQ) Development

When we're feeling overwhelmed with emotions, it's easy to go on autopilot to satisfy our primal urges and react on impulse. Reacting impulsively in the moment is like that temporary satisfaction you get when scratching that itch. But that scratch has now left a mark, and the itchiness has become worse, requiring even more scratching. Suddenly, you're left dealing with an open wound.

There's a concrete link between emotional intelligence and job performance[xii]. Just like giving in to emotions and acting on impulse is the easy way out, it's also the fastest way to lose respect as a sales leader and make your job incredibly more difficult—that is if your impulses haven't led to your termination.

Making decisions and reacting to tense issues under pressure calls for leaders to have a high degree of emotional Intelligence (EQ). When empathy, as discussed earlier, is a top-five element of EQ, it helps ground sales leaders. The other four elements that sales leaders can develop to increase EQ are self-regulation, self-awareness, social awareness, and motivation.

Emotional self-regulation is the ability to control emotions. Leaders who are thoughtful, or make a conscious effort to be thoughtful, develop this core EQ element[xiii]. Reappraisal is a technique that has worked for me and others[xiv]. Stepping back from the moment and looking at the big picture, reappraisal forces you to reinterpret an event to broaden your perspective.

We all know people in our lives who aren't self-aware and how mind boggling their hypocritical comments can be. Strong sales leaders are sensitive to that; they are acutely aware of their shortcomings, work on weaknesses, and lean on their strengths. People with high EQ have developed their emotional *self-awareness*[xv]. They recognize that they are role models and as such, they must act with integrity. Because they understand their emotions, they are better equipped at preventing their feelings from taking over.

Solid social awareness is what I refer to as the polishing element of EQ. You can be the most self-aware person with a high degree of emotional self-regulation, but if you're not an effective communicator, it simply won't translate. Sales leaders with solid social skills look to bring people together through communication, hone in on bonding subject matter, and are mindful not to dominate conversations, allowing the voices of others to shine. They can manage disputes, influence the conversation toward the positive, and offer input that is neutral or unoffensive. Social awareness is a crucial EQ skill [xvi].

The last element of EQ is *self-motivation*. With motivation comes resilience, tolerance, and perspective. Highly motivated sales leaders look at the long-term effects of decisions, and consciously avoid actions that only have an immediate impact. Motivation provides the energy to do the right things and to take the high road rather than take the easy way out. Motivation is contagious and influences those around them to follow their leader.

Developing these core elements in order to increase EQ is an ongoing task. Sales leaders will be tested emotionally—they are the heads of their own micro-environment, the presidents of their own complaint departments. Dealing with issues objectively and without giving in to feelings reduces long term consequences for short term results. Sales leaders that continually strive for a high EQ will earn the respect of their team, be more effective at their post, and retain the professionalism their position requires. EQ is essential for sales leaders, without it, they have no business leading teams.

Technology offers new avenues in accelerating the honing of interpersonal skills and the development of EQ. Mursion, for example, offers Virtual Reality (VR) interpersonal simulations where participants learn by doing in a controlled and safe environment so that mistakes become lessons without the consequences normally experienced in the real world. Skeptical about the efficacy of VR simulations? The Stanford University's Virtual Human Interaction Lab, and Columbia University's School of Social Work have empirical proof that VR training is indeed sticky, especially as it pertains to behavioral change. On empathy, for example, the results of thousands of participants are being studied on the impact of an ongoing empathy experiment high-lighted in the twelve-minute Virtual Reality film of acclaim recently screened at the Tribeca Film Festival, *1000 Cut Journey*. Professional sports and the U.S. military have been using immersive technology for years, and it's finally making its way into the corporate world.

Measuring Staff: How Do You Do it?

If it can't be measured, it's just aspirational. Real goals are measurable, and sales leaders must carefully design a framework that clearly illustrates progress towards team member goals. With the distractions and potential chaos of day-to-day sales, it's important for sales reps to focus on the right things. Sales leaders use dashboards and leaderboards to this end. For the sales leader, the right design identifies measurable behavior and impact in order to acknowledge the attributes of top performers as well as identify reps that are struggling that need assistance.

We've established that sales reps are competitive. They want to know where they stand. This is another reason sales leaders use dashboards and leaderboards. A dashboard is a quick reference to how the sales individual and team are progressing towards their goals. What is being measured should be aligned with the company's goals, and it should also be as objective as possible.

There are a multitude of ways to design a dashboard. What I've found works best is a 3x3x3 format. In this design, the category headings should be Activities, Objectives, and Results. Under each category should be a tracking value that is updated in real time or frequently. For instance, if this is a call center, tracking number of dials may be an activity that merits inclusion. Under objectives, that call activity can have a color-coded indicator that shows how the rep is tracking. Under results, actual progress to the goal for the period is indicated with a graphic that also displays pay level based on amount of goal achieved. After experimenting with many variations and different formats, this framework has worked best for me and those I've worked with.

Rudimentary Dashboard Mockup:

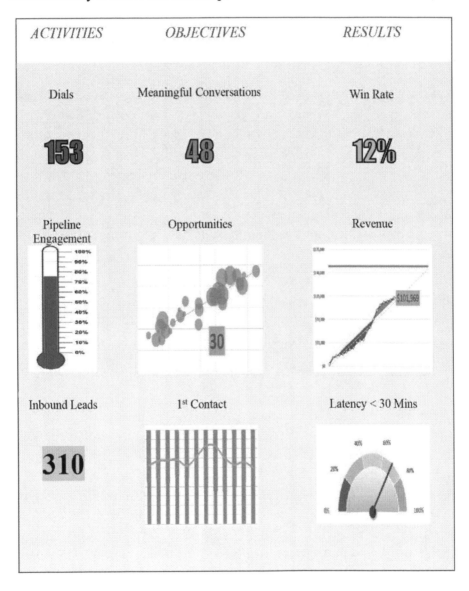

Leaderboards are sort of like score cards that the entire office can see displayed openly. Leaderboards may stack rank sales reps who are performing best based on objectives also found in the dashboard. They may also be specific to a promotion or a product. They can be designed to track the performance ranking of a sales contest. A host of information can be used on leaderboards to motivate sales staff to be competitive. The key is to ensure the information reported is updated frequently and is accurate, or else the leaderboard concept will backfire when disgruntled reps discredit its reliability.

Make Data and Intuition Your Allies

Just as sales reps have influence on whether a product or service sells, sales leaders have tremendous influence on goals. They have influence on how realistic a goal is during the planning phase. They have influence on the rollout of those goals with their direct reports.

Sales reps want to know the rationale behind sales goals as well. Bear in mind, reps may be coming off a banner year where they gave all they could to meet their previous goal or had an unusual sale that boost their performance over target. An increase over their best year may seem unfathomable. Because a large portion of compensation is tied to achieving goals, sales reps are sensitive to the topic. That's why the biggest sales challenge is getting sales reps to believe in their goals. A sales leader must be able to prove the goals are realistic, achievable with effort, and can be exceeded under the right circumstances. It also means painting a picture of what is possible long term.

Drawing upon comparable territories is an effective technique I've used in the past. First, take a remote, low populated area with a relatively high sales volume and determining per capita sales. That information can then be extrapolated to other territories to show potential.

Competitors in an area that dominate market share is another way to show potential. Data that correlates to product or service usage and paints a clear picture on market potential is another effective use of data. Reps are put at ease when they hear more about the marketing plans, such as how much advertising spend they can expect in their territory, any corporate-driven special events, promotions to move the needle, or new product launches. All of this information can be used to back sales reps off the cliff and convince them of their goals, even when the economy is soft.

Where does intuition come in? It begins during the planning phase when the sales leader's boss floats the high-level company sales goal which has probably been conjured up through *spreadsheet management*. Does it sound like a stretch goal that is achievable, a soft goal that underutilizes the team leaving money on the table, or pie in the sky? Data can blind us to how our customers actually feel and act, and sales leaders must be attuned to this possibility.

As a sales leader, find out what is happening internally to get to that number. Then weigh that against market intelligence that only those in the field are privy to. For example, if the biggest client is predicted to be insolvent, a competitor is aggressively attacking a flag ship product with a new release, or the buying trend in the marketplace is changing, those are important factors to weigh in. Intelligence from the field that should be considered may also have positive indicators, such as a prospect list with large viable potential customers expected to land soon, anticipated new year orders, or expected uptick in business from the best clients.

Intuition and data are also intermingled when it comes to sales coaching. Often, when a sales rep falls to the bottom of a leaderboard, the sales leader intuitively reacts and gets the sales rep trained up in the suspected sales gap area. The skill development may indeed be lacking, but it may not be commensurate to what the top salespeople have in their repertoire and what makes them so much more successful. Weaving in data analytics as part of the business development plan forces sales leaders to have purpose and be objective about what they measure[xvii]. The sales leader should observe in detail the performance of the top-producing reps in the company, and then run regression analyses in order to clarify the characteristics that have the greatest impact among the top sales reps. Good sales leaders will use the balance of intuition as a gauge and objective data to inform them on the best way to make improvements with staff in order to reach their full potential.

The Secret to Becoming a Well-Respected Sales Leader

Ever since I was first promoted from sales representative to a sales leadership role, I've tried to become the leader I would admire if I remained as an individual contributor.

Taking my own experience into account and speaking with others who climbed the career ladder to executive positions, I've come to the consensus that after proving sales acumen as a top performing sales representative the next steps to becoming a truly respected sales leader among the entire sales staff are leading by example, listening sincerely to your team members, and maintaining a high level of integrity.

Leadership by example means a lot more than showing a sales rep that they can sell a product or service because you just did it yourself. In fact, that approach can backfire, especially when the sales leader stacks the cards in their favor with primed customers or easy targets. The takeaway then for the sales staff is that the sales leader "thinks he's better than us." Instead, leadership by example means never asking any salesperson to do what you wouldn't do yourself in their position. It means rolling up your sleeves at the risk of embarrassing yourself to learn what your team members have to experience daily. Your team members will respect you for the effort and honest attempt.

Sales representatives have a lot to say, and many can be extremely creative. The trick is separating the petty and personal from the enterprise conversations that may move the needle. Those discussions that qualify need to be taken seriously because they may greatly impact the growth of the business, improve upon existing conditions to help overall sales performance, and at the very least make the rep feel empowered. Listening without distraction, taking notes, and asking questions illustrates your willingness during the conversation. Most importantly, following up with the sales representative or sales manager after the conversation is paramount, even if the follow up is a decision against the proposed improvement. As a third step, regardless of whether it's adopted or not, give credit for the idea to the person. Under no circumstance should the sales leader take credit for someone else's idea. That's the fastest way to lose credibility.

Here it is in action.

At the multinational company where we were experiencing accelerated sales growth, we had a large number of creative reps, so we assembled an advisory council comprised of these reps. They would also speak on behalf of certain reps in their region and give credit where due.

This group would meet twice a year and bring issues and proposed solutions to our attention for consideration. Usually, we adopted some of the proposed solutions at least in part. But one time, everything was truly in left field. The issues were not really things that required attention since we had proof they were exaggerated. The proposals were unrealistic (and costly).

The advice I received was to stay quiet and not address any of it. Instead, I reached out individually to each person who was credited with raising the issue and explained as tactfully as I could the reason the issue wasn't on the radar and why we would not be implementing that solution. The response was a genuine appreciation that I took the time to explain and seriously consider what was proposed.

A Note on Integrity

The most challenging component to being a well-respected leader is maintaining a high level of integrity. This means holding everyone to the same standards. It means taking the high road when your emotions tell you otherwise. It means making some really, really hard decisions based on core values, some of which may cost you your job. It means putting your team and the company first even if you have to let someone go that you like personally but just isn't meeting performance standards.

As head of sales for a tech startup, we gained significant traction after transforming customer service reps into a high performing inside sales team. Another round of funding was on the horizon and the Founders decided to experiment with a new sales initiative that had the potential to bring in exponential sales numbers. While the upside was appealing, it dramatically extended the sales cycle, was unaligned with sales fundamentals, and unaligned with our supply side of the marketplace. We all felt the need to create the hockey stick of growth most appealing to investors, but I felt compelled to take a measured approach to this pivot. The jobs of the sales staff would be greatly impacted and the organization would be missing out on bread and butter sales from a core customer group with the change.

The person who had some success with the new strategy during the early experimental phase was thrown into a sales operations role from a marketing function and eventually took over our best members of the sales team. This move killed the high performing and collaborative culture I had worked hard to build over the past year, made others who were not part of this group feel inferior, and unraveled the sales fundamentals that had previously been working so well. Sales reps feared for their jobs, and there were murmurs that some may be leaving given the uncertainty. I expressed my concerns to a company Founder several times while working to mitigate the risks of the new directive. In the end I was forced out of the organization.

By leading by example, listening intently, and doing my best to maintain a high level of integrity, I've earned the trust of every sales team I've been a part of in my career. I truly care for those I work with; I want them to succeed and go on to do great things. Knowing that I've had some influence in their success is gratifying. And that's the final lesson here: you lead by example, listen to your people, and maintain a high level of integrity because ultimately it makes you feel good to help others while capturing value for the organization by inciting a ripple effect—if you embody these positive leadership traits, your team members will usually pass them along and influence others to do so as well.

Really Showing Up: Advocating for Your Team

Good sales leaders should know who they've got on their team. Take more of an interest in them than anyone else is. Know their skills, experience, and how they can be leveraged to help other team members who may be lacking in areas. Sales leaders should have a pulse on personal events that may impact the job such as a childbirth or death in the family, expectations should be adjusted accordingly. Above all, sales leaders should be looking for things reps are doing right to influence upwards, provide acknowledgements in front of coworkers, and frequently acknowledge reps in front of upper management when appropriate.

Remember that sales performance data speaks volumes. When sales reps are continuously crushing it, sales leaders should extend the positive by reiterating the biggest victories when around people in the organization with significant influence. Leaderboards and dashboards offer transparency, especially within management.

That means sales leaders need to be prepared to address questions about underperforming reps as well. Know the root cause of performance lag. Know what is being done to course correct. Know how accepting the rep is of the situation. Be optimistic without blowing smoke. And be neutral and factual when the rep is pushing back or making matters worse. Never throw direct reports under the bus—that includes not mentioning idiosyncrasies that paint a negative picture. Instead they should advocate and rally on behalf of their struggling team member. If the sales leader has faith that the rep can turn performance around, then that should be the theme for everyone else in the organization.

A team is only as strong as its weakest member.

In instances when there is continuous underperformance, insubordination, and conflict with reps, sales leaders should identify if a life event (e.g. divorce) is a possible cause and take that into consideration before holding the rep accountable. Sometimes the rep just isn't the right fit to perform at a high caliber relative to the sales context. When there's ongoing conflict or overt insubordination (e.g. rep refuses to use the CRM), steps need to be taken to begin the termination process. Keeping someone on who's substandard jeopardizes the team and sends bad optics for the rest of the group.

A big part of the sales leader's job is to protect the company. At times that means getting people off the team and replacing them with people that can perform at or above standard. Having said that, everyone deserves a fair chance, the sales leader should remain benevolent. Reps that are struggling should be given verbal warnings (all documented), provided support for help, and three chances to course correct with tangible binary goals to be reviewed after a specific period such as thirty days.

If goals still aren't met, two subsequent write ups are in order with modified goals. If the rep is still not meeting standard, the sales manager must terminate. The exception to this is when there's a new hire and important milestones aren't met within the first ninety days to six months. In that case, the termination process can be accelerated. The important thing is the rep should not be surprised by the termination decision. Sales leaders must accept that accountability is paramount and necessary!

A Note on Terminations

I've never come across a sales leader who enjoyed terminating employees. Being terminated sucks. Doing the termination sucks too.

Sales leaders delivering the information to the rep should be accompanied by a coworker who has expertise such as Human Resources (HR) or a manager with termination experience (preferably one that has been personally terminated in the past themselves). The conversation should be factual, direct, and the phrase, "this decision is final", should be used. Sales leaders should leave no doubt about the decision, and as much as it may feel like positive aspects about the rep should be communicated, this is not the time to bring those up, it will quickly devolve into a debate over the decision to terminate. Reactions are unpredictable but if the sales rep has been properly warned as already described, it mitigates the potential for an explosive emotional reaction, and if everything is documented as suggested, it reduces the chances of an unlawful termination suit. Just to be clear, everything should be above board anyway. The terminated employee should be advised on what to do with the company property, who will be in touch, and when everything should be expected to be finished.

Even the most secure reps become a bit unhinged when a colleague is terminated. I'm an advocate of having the reps' direct supervisor involved until the end and having an open-door policy about speaking with reps regarding the termination. Depending on the company policy, conversations should be kept at a high level without disparagement. There are companies that discourage speaking about terminations at all, no announcements, no attention given whatsoever.

At such a company, I was actually ordered by a Founder not to inform the staff when sales professionals (or anyone else) left the company, which became a cluster because internal resources would find out the hard way after the employee was not responding to requests. Absence of information begets suspicion. The best way to quash the rumor mill is with quick and credible information—address the topic head on and then move on[xviii]!

For the terminated employee, termination can be a traumatic event. HR or someone in the company should have information to help soften the blow. This information should include benefits options, what can be expected when a future employer calls, resume advice, and job board help. Some companies offer placement services which can be a blessing. Most of the time the rep was just not a fit for the sales context, and probably will be a top salesperson elsewhere. In the end, the terminated rep and the company are better off.

Managing Frequent Change

Change is inevitable, though many sales professionals who feel they have cracked the code to success in the present sales environment will resist anything that disrupts their formula. To manage change effectively, the focus should be on people and process.

Sales leaders need to ask many questions on behalf of staff before change occurs and preemptively compile answers that can be presented as an FAQ reference for internal staff affected by the change.

On process changes, visuals such as flow charts, text documents, and a coaching plan to reinforce things one on one should be provided when introducing the change to the broader group.

Sales leaders should convey to the team the positive impact of realizing the vision not only for the company, but for the improvement of individual salespeople. When new skills are required, explain how that makes staff more valuable and how much the company is spending on their development. Invite people to work in small teams of three that balances strengths among team members to increase the chances of quicker change adoption. Most importantly, underscore the silver lining and look for the positive throughout the transition.

Spouses and Significant Others

Field sales reps spend a considerable amount of time on the road and away from loved ones. The sacrifices and burden of their absence is felt with their loved ones. Inside sales handles a disproportionate amount of abusive calls, and at times may bring the stress of work back home. Both types of sales professionals are physically and mentally committing themselves to their roles at high emotional and personal costs. Those closest to them recognize it the most.

When opportunities arise to meet or speak with spouses and significant others, sales leaders should make a conscious effort to show appreciation and respect. They should remind themselves that the loved one is not a company employee, but rather a concerned partner. Thank them for their patience and understanding, and, when they have complaints, listen to them without offering suggestions.

There are a couple of things I've done in the past that have helped me personally with spouses and significant others. First, I keep an updated list of names. Referring to the spouse of your direct report by the wrong name is a bad error. Referring to a trusted list can save sales leaders from personal damage and embarrassment.

The other thing that has worked for me when mingling with spouses and significant others is offering acknowledgements. This takes the form of acknowledging some major and nuanced victories of the employee and how that helped the rest of the team or people at the company. Acknowledgment of the integrity of the employee, or other values the employee demonstrates. Also, acknowledgment of support by the significant other or spouse, because without support at home, sales professionals will not be able to function properly.

Sales Leader "To Do" List

So, where do we go from here? What do we do with all this information we've absorbed on leadership this chapter? In the spirit of action, I've designed the following sales leader "to do" list that I hope you will find effective in your leadership journey.

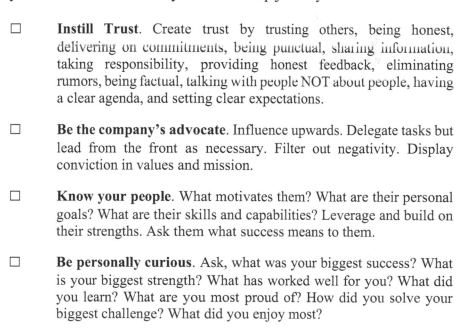

☐   **Instill Trust**. Create trust by trusting others, being honest, delivering on commitments, being punctual, sharing information, taking responsibility, providing honest feedback, eliminating rumors, being factual, talking with people NOT about people, having a clear agenda, and setting clear expectations.

☐   **Be the company's advocate**. Influence upwards. Delegate tasks but lead from the front as necessary. Filter out negativity. Display conviction in values and mission.

☐   **Know your people**. What motivates them? What are their personal goals? What are their skills and capabilities? Leverage and build on their strengths. Ask them what success means to them.

☐   **Be personally curious**. Ask, what was your biggest success? What is your biggest strength? What has worked well for you? What did you learn? What are you most proud of? How did you solve your biggest challenge? What did you enjoy most?

☐   **One-on-one meetings: be intentional and prescriptive.** [a)] Kick off the conversation with something positive. [b)] Set an inspiring agenda tailored to the rep's values or situation. [c)] Address room for improvement and get commitment. [d)] Agree on goals. [e)] Collaborate on developing an action plan.

☐   **Correct perceptions.** When they display low self-esteem, encourage them. If they are arrogant or out of touch, ask them to provide factual proof. When they are blind to weakness, make them see ("I have noticed . . ."). When they see weakness as strength, ask the reason they feel that way and provide insight for correction.

Leadership Principles

As we leave this key chapter, we're leaving with a plethora of tales, techniques, and takeaways. With that in mind, let's simplify things around the subject, and with a simple list of leadership principles. While everything we've covered in this chapter is important, if you can remember and enact these ten principles in your professional journey, you'll be doing yourself, your company, and your career a real service.

I.   Ask more of yourself than others expect.

II.   Ask more of your team members than anyone else would.

III.   Take a greater personal interest in your team members than anyone else would.

IV.   Empower your team members, give them space to do their job.

V.   Say "WE" not "I"—you succeed or fail together.

VI.   Your team works with you not for you.

VII.   Be mindful of team morale.

VIII.   Keep team members informed.

IX.   Treat everyone with dignity.

X.   Respect and support your team members.

CHAPTER 9

A Practical Guide to Team Building

For the uninitiated, team building is an essential part of creating a world class sales organization. Because it requires investments in time and resources, upper management may not see the value of taking sales staff out of the field or off the phones in order for them to frolic on a team-building excursion. This is where the executive sales leader needs to sell the benefits of team building to get buy-in from bosses and coworkers.

At its core, team building tackles the problem of employee disengagement, which is costly for businesses. In fact, a relatively recent Gallup report estimated the cost of such loses to be $550 billion annually in the U.S.[xix]. Disengaged employees are less productive and experience greater absenteeism. When staff is all under one roof, there is risk of disengagement if leadership isn't sensitive to that risk.

For sales professionals in the field, that risk grows in magnitude because those employees are detached physically from coworkers and left to operate on their own virtual islands. A Gallup metadata study shows engaged employees are more productive, with publicly traded organizations with highly engaged employees outperforming less engaged workforces by 147 percent earnings per share[xx]. Team building addresses issues of disengagement before they become too costly by fostering employee engagement.

Let's take it a bit further even. According to *Forbes*, "Team Building is the best investment you can make.[xxi]" The benefits of team building are numerous. Among them are increased collaboration, reduced conflict, and better communication. Team building breaks down silos and encourages employee bonding. When done right, team building creates shared memories and experiences that employees reflect on during good times and bad. Team building attracts and retains talent, smart businesses use it as a marketing and recruitment tool.

Companies that make strategic investments in employee development are 11 percent more profitable and twice as likely to retain employees, according to another Gallup study[xxii]. When the organization makes an investment in team building, it sends a positive message to staff that they are appreciated . . . but it *has to actually be team building!*

The concept of team building varies across organizations. I have to admit, most of what I've seen elsewhere is definitely not qualified as team building.

Setting aside a day to play board games with staff, not team building.

Going on a picnic together isn't team building.

Staying on a beachfront property with coworkers for a day or two of drinking and debauchery isn't team building and is probably grounds for termination.

Team building cannot be a half-hearted attempt to bring folks together outside of normal working conditions. Team building has to be planned methodically and executed purposely. In addition to sunk costs for pulling people off their normal jobs, the company is allocating a portion of budget that can be used for more tangible business expenses to pay for team building. It's a big investment, and it had better be done right! Sales leaders should treat team building with the seriousness and professionalism it merits, as if it were being financed from their own pockets.

Team Building to Create a Powerful Sales Force

Underscoring the importance of working together, shared values, and group development leads to a powerful sales force. Allow me to explain with the following real-life experiences.

When I was first promoted from a sales rep to a leadership role, I already knew that we had some skilled salespeople. I also knew we all worked independently of each other. Some were technically superior. Others had better hunting skills. And some were better at growing existing businesses. As we hired to support extremely aggressive growth plans, I knew the missing component was to have a sales force that was a *team*.

I started on that goal by having a sales meeting for the West Coast reps in Moab. We were on a shoestring budget. With only six of us at the time, we rented an RV and headed for the outdoors. We had great enterprise conversations on the four-hour drive from Salt Lake City to Moab. During our three-day retreat, we had agenda items that we went into with great detail, including how to tackle the sales goals, what was working best for each rep, and a training session so we were armed when we came back to civilization. This was offset with extracurriculars designed to encourage working together.

On a whitewater rafting excursion, I wanted to illustrate the difference between working as a team and working as individuals. I entered the raft with one of the reps in a calm part of the Colorado River and we sat with our backs toward each other. We tried to paddle for five minutes but went nowhere. It was actually hysterical, two grown men paddling frantically yet going nowhere, and the lesson was not lost on the reps. We had a great time from there on out. More important, we all worked as a team, leveraging each other's strengths and helping each other achieve goals to become the dominant region.

When I became VP of Sales, the regions (East, West, and Canada) had their own teams and subculture. We were also growing from a small company in North America to a midsized company; things were becoming more formalized and many of the early hires were starting to feel disconnected. My objective was to have one team regardless of Sales Director or region.

The entire field sales team met outside of Phoenix at a large property that would serve as our retreat. There were only a third of the beds we needed, and nobody was permitted to share a bed due to company rules. The alternative were barracks-style cots squeezed in throughout the property. I created a series of competitions based on policy and product knowledge where those who finished at the top of the list were able to pick their sleeping arrangements. It became much more about pride than rest, and immediately it set the tone for our culture discussions.

Although we did cover new product launches, best practices, and sales objectives, we primarily focused on the foundations of building a solid team for the future. I acted as a moderator as the reps debated and eventually agreed on our core values, minimum standards that each sales rep should meet, and a detailed list of sales rep responsibilities broken down to time allocation requirements. Having these in place after the retreat forced other reps to become custodians of their own team. It made it clear what they had to be accountable to and that this was something they came up with rather than top down mandates. It also meant the onus was on veteran sales reps to help new hires meet standard. In the end everyone seemed to take ownership and those few that were struggling stepped up with their performance and commitment to the team.

We ended up doing a few team building activities, the most formal of which was close-quarter battle training at an indoor facility with acclaimed instructors. We used actual handguns that discharged paint cartridges, and the walls were on pulleys so they were constantly being changed.

After learning the fundamentals of the shooting platform and how to work together to clear a room, the reps were put into teams where they had to compete against the instructors. At first, they were getting decimated. As they worked more effectively as a team, they ended up beating the instructors and successfully clearing the rooms. The lesson went much further than the range since that activity alone created an unbreakable bond that lasted several years between the reps who were there.

With values and standards established, there was a sense of purpose that could be built upon by incorporating technical product knowledge with sales skills development and marketing initiatives. That would require a minimum of five full days of training and help from the Marketing department. After creating our first curriculum and sharing it with our VP of Marketing, he dubbed it the name that we would use going forward—Monster Training!

Our sales staff was growing as was our product offering, so for Monster Training we would have everyone meet outside of Las Vegas at our training facility. The gathering would take place about halfway through the year, so we would include sales performance into the overall tally along with team games and individual games to test product and policy knowledge.

After those first few fierce competitive hours, an atmosphere of camaraderie emerged. With a limited budget, I was in charge of getting provisions, cooking, doing most of the cleaning, and ensuring every-one was acting appropriately. We spent all hours together either at the house or at the training center. Eventually our sales force got so large we had to rent side by side mansions to support the size of Monster Training.

Monster Training was a highly anticipated event that differentiated us, though it was the team we established as a result that was what our customers and even our competition most often praised. It actually helped retain talent and draw in new talent. There is no doubt that we became the most highly trained, most motivated, and highest-performing sales force in the industry during that period. Putting in the time, effort, and resources to build a true team pays dividends for many years into the future.

How to Devise Real Team Building

Monster Training worked amazingly well for us. But what about for you and your organization?

When designing team building events, start by selecting no more than three primary objectives. Those objectives will inform the type of activities and venue for the team building. Budget, time allocation, and interest are all parameters for option consideration. Once a list of options is whittled down to half a dozen or less, other sales leaders, HR employees, or other folks at the company who best understand the team's interests, should weigh-in before getting into planning particulars.

Let's put this thought exercise into practice.

Say we have a hypothetical sales staff of inside and outside sales professionals who are disjointed and accustomed to working independently. Sales operations has determined that inside sales should work lower volume remote accounts for outside sales, and outside sales should work closely with inside sales to ensure they are fully abreast of opportunities or potential account issues. Therefore, the objectives for the team building event are effective communication and collaboration.

Next, we tease out venue options based on what we have to work with. For the sake of argument, let's assume we have thirty sales professionals, including twenty-five reps and five sales directors. Due to scheduling conflicts, seasonality as it pertains to business, and personal obligations, we can only pull everyone out of the field or off their regular jobs for two days including travel time. That allots only one day of fully dedicated team building. After travel expenses and usual payroll costs, the budget is restricted to $350 per person or $10,500 for team building specific activities.

Based on time of year, interests, flight availability, and flexibility, Seattle has been selected as the location for the team building event. After receiving input from trusted coworkers, the agenda looks something like this:

Day 1 (Thursday)

Time	Who	Activity
11 a.m.	Sales Leaders (SL)	Arrive SeaTac, review and confirm logistics for the day
12:30 p.m.	Group 1 (G1) & Group 2 (G2)	Arrive @ SeaTac Airport
1 p.m.	G1 & G2 + two SLs	Pike Place Market for lunch & informal walking tour
1:15 p.m.	Group 3 (G3)	Arrive @ SeaTac Airport

1:45 p.m.	G3 + a SL	Pike Place Market for quick lunch & informal walking tour
2 p.m.	Group 4 & Group 5	Arrive @ SeaTac Airport
2:30 p.m.	G4 & G5 + SLs	Pike Place Market for quick snack & informal condensed tour
3 p.m.	G1, G2, G3 + SLs	Meet at the original Starbucks
3:45 p.m.	All	Rendezvous @ Seattle Spheres
4 p.m.	All	Amazon neighborhood informal walking tour
5 p.m.	All	Escape room
7:30 p.m.	All	Casual Dinner @ Emerald Downs
9 p.m.	All	Hotel check-in

Day 2 (Friday)

Time	Who	Activity
Before 7:30 a.m.	Open to all	Breakfast per company policy
7:30 a.m.	All	Company Knowledge activity
8:30 a.m.	All	Teams assigned; team name and brand activity
9:45 a.m.	All	Break

10:15 a.m.	All	Square Challenge activity
11:30 a.m.	All	Lunch (catered)
12:30 p.m.	All	Figure simulation
1:45 p.m.	All	Break
2:15 p.m.	All	Communication styles
4 p.m.	All	Defined roles and wrap-up
5:45 p.m.	G1 - G5	Dropped off at SeaTac airport
6:00 p.m.	SLs	Team Building postmortem @ 13 Coins restaurant
8:00 p.m.	SLs	Depart for home

Before I attempt to decipher the agenda matrices, we need to iron out some additional logistical information, such as who and when are rental cars being picked up, which sales leaders are in charge of which groups, who is checking flight status, and various contingency plans (e.g. arriving flight delayed so rep must meet us at Starbucks, Seattle Spheres, escape room, or Emerald Downs depending on the arrival time). Thoughtful planning is imperative!

If you check the statistics for on-time arrivals on websites when booking flights, mornings have less delay than later in the day. Since the venue is on the West Coast, reps from the East Coast should take early morning first flights out (G1 & G2). Traveling earliest and furthest, they will also be hungry when they arrive, so they should be fed proper meals, and allocating time for full lunches is advised. Midwest regions should book early morning flights in their time zone (G3). Followed by West (G4 & G5). When departing, flight delays work in favor of the agenda and can provide a welcome buffer.

Why was Pike Place Market picked? Well, it's a cool place! Also, it's teeming with business, people from all walks of life selling goods, and it's an opportunity to watch fishmongers communicate and coordinate while they literally toss fish around in front of you.

The First Starbucks. Love it or hate it, Starbucks is a case study in successful businesses that have revolutionized the market. Prior to the visit, sales leaders conducting these tours should have talking points and goals for each location, including the first Starbucks. There should be subtle lessons that apply to the reps' lives and that underscore the importance of communication and coordination.

Amazon. Who hasn't purchased something from Amazon? This is a good talking point for friends and family at home, plus it demonstrates how a business can go from nothing to a behemoth with a campus that has taken over a chunk of Seattle that was mostly an unfavorable part of town. Use it as a good discussion on the pros and cons of gentrification.

Escape Room. This is where the groups get split into teams so they each have a specific escape room designated for the challenge. The teams should consist of people that will work together such as inside and outside sales reps working accounts in the same territories. It provides an environment that forces the team to work together to escape. Winners are rewarded by being first in line to check in at the hotel later that evening.

Emerald Downs. Less about horse racing and more about having a casual dinner with colleagues. It is a clean racetrack with a lively atmosphere that encourages people to root for their favorite horses and relax without pressure after a long day. It also happens to be the place where I had the best crème brulee of my life, so I'm biased.

Open breakfast. With little chance to acclimate to the time zone, East Coasters will rise much earlier than everyone else, so an open schedule for breakfast allows flexibility to accommodate everyone's needs.

Company knowledge activity. Designed to break the ice and encourage participation from everyone, this activity is for all present. Individuals are given points and stack ranked on a whiteboard for the rest of the day as bragging rights by answering general knowledge questions about the company. The question is asked, and there are ninety seconds to write down the answer. The facilitator (usually me, maybe you!) then verifies who answered correctly, gives credit, and an explanation of the answer, including history or backstory. Questions and answers usually lead to discussions and reinforce company knowledge. The activity reminds everyone that they are all part of the same organization and share with its evolution. The activity is designed to bond people together.

Team name and brand activity. Teams are formed, sales leaders oversee specific teams as micro facilitators for the team. The teams are made up of individuals who will be working with each other during normal business. In this activity, they need to agree on a team name and corresponding logo they can be proud of.

Square challenge. Team members are blindfolded and work together to create a square using a long rope. This activity promotes collaboration and communication.

Figure simulation. Teams each designate one person as the representative. Those selected are taken into a private space away from everyone where they have two minutes to write down details of the figure their team will replicate using universal interlocking plastic bricks. No photos are allowed, of course. The spokesperson returns and communicates the vision. Everyone gets a chance to be spokesperson. The team with the figure that most closely resembles the example, wins. This activity encourages communication and collaboration.

Communication styles. This begins as an individual activity, and the sales leaders should also participate individually. Using an assessment questionnaire that diagnoses which style each participant falls into, break up the room into the different styles and have the people who scored under each style congregate into a designated part of the room, facing in toward the other groups. A spokesperson (other than a sales leader) uses a marker and notepad with easel or something similar to describe likes and dislikes for communicating with their group. The facilitator summarizes how best to communicate with each person and what to avoid based on their communication style.

Defined roles and wrap-up. The facilitator interjects the reality of tomorrow into the activities and how they have developed skills to work better together. Specific call outs should be mentioned as proof and acknowledgments from the activities of the event. The facilitator should clearly iterate what "good" looks like in their functions and define their roles and responsibilities. This should include a Q & A. Participants should leave having an understanding of how the team building has helped them be better communicators and collaborators, having a closer bond, and understanding what they will be held accountable to.

Post Mortem at 13 Coins. It is important to strike while the iron is hot after a group event. I've found creativity is at its peak at that time, and areas for improvement are fresh on the mind. It also allows some decompression and bonding with sales leaders after enduring an action-packed two days. Picking a restaurant near the airport helps calm departure nerves as well.

What to Avoid

The initial stages of planning team building events gives one freedom to go in different directions. That being said, a few simple things should be avoided from the beginning.

Timing is important. The end of the quarter when some sales reps need every waking hour to make goal is not a good time to book an event that pulls reps out of their territories. Time of year is also a consideration. Is it seasonally busy in your industry? If so, pick a time of year that is slow.

Companies often use employee personal days to get large groups from across the country into a single location for team building. The thought is it avoids disrupting normal business. This is a mistake! Avoid weekends and holidays as well. Employees will be more focused and less disgruntled when they don't have to give up personal days. If there's no other option than having employees travel over a holiday or during a weekend (it happens) it's important for sales leaders to reach out directly and ask permission in advance. Call to see if the participant would be kind enough to travel on a personal day in order to accommodate the company.

Be mindful of team groupings. Partner people who will be working together after the event. Also partner the proper sales leaders to act as facilitator assistants with the right groups based on personality, skills, and relationships. There is a science to doing this right that goes even deeper. Author David Logan suggests assembling teams in groups of three in a strategic manner is most effective[xxiii]. The triad should have a mentor or influencer, the person responsible for the quality of the relationship of the other two. They should have a common interest and shared values. If we think about how we connect through LinkedIn, we find similarity. It's one-on-one connection based on a third common connection with bonding interests. The triad design is an effective way to group people during team building and during normal business.

Team Building for Small Teams

There were seven of us covering the West and I was the sales leader in charge of the group. We had just brought on two new hires that had much different backgrounds than the rest of the group. There was a need to have the new hires feel welcomed, and to leverage the diversity they brought to our team. We were all fairly strong willed, so I had to be careful on potential personality conflicts.

Triads were formed balancing the veteran staff members with new hires whenever we were doing activities separately or not traveling together. With that configuration in mind, we switched the new hires halfway through our event so everyone could benefit from working together.

To cap off the team building, I was excited about a sailing activity I had planned. Team members would be able to learn the basics of operating a sailboat and by working together we could make it together to our destination across the bay to Angel Island. What was described in the marketing collateral for the excursion and what transpired were completely different. The captain/instructor was reticent to give us the autonomy we expected. He did show us some sailing basics and allowed each of us to be at the helm, but it was hardly an action-packed ride, more of a leisure cruise. That was an expensive lesson for me both from a budget standpoint and from a credibility standpoint. From that day forward I confirmed in great detail exactly what we should be getting before exposing my team and wasting company money. The good thing about this sailing excursion is while we were waiting to launch, a rep from our group who was always selling, struck a deal with the marina that ended up more than offsetting the costs of our excursion. That and it was a beautiful day on the water to share with our crew.

Team Building Across Departments

Companies with growing departments eventually become siloed. That's a major factor in employee disengagement, and it can create an adversarial atmosphere between departments.

As we grew into a midsized company, it was apparent that we were falling into that same trap. My coworker, the CFO, had recently thrown out the idea of participating in my next team building event, which I welcomed of course. When I suggested that we do something for the company that would involve different departments, he was all in.

We agreed it would need to be late summer or early autumn, before things kicked into high gear in Q4. He also suggested we treat the group to some sightseeing (nice to have the head of finance driving the planning ideas). After going down a list of locations and options, we settled on doing the Ragnar in Napa Valley, a roughly 200-mile-long California road race.

It was January, and I announced the company team building event at our national sales meeting, followed by a company email that encouraged any participants interested to volunteer. Within a week, we had more volunteers than we budgeted for. Though after I connected individually with all those interested and told them the rigors of doing the Ragnar, we went from worrying we'd have to turn people away, to wondering if we'd have enough participants.

Still, we pulled enough people together to field the teams we needed. In addition to organizing the travel logistics and booking two large passenger vans for the event, I was on the hook to have everything prepared, so the team only had to focus on where they needed to be to run and cheer each other on. In each van I included a folder that contained a breakdown of each leg of the run, and a colored map of each leg of the course, including specific details on distance, elevation, and level of difficulty. We had an estimated time to meet between teams at the end of leg six, twelve, eighteen, thirty, and at the finish line based on individual running pace. When one team was running, the other was resting in their van or at the hotel.

We decorated each van to represent our company and our team. The vans were outfitted with supplies. Reflective vests, strobes, and headlamps for night runs were part of a care package I provided each participant. The van had a supply of nutritional food and liquid. For prep and recovery each van had foam rollers, message sticks, and yoga mats. Everything they could possibly need in the duration required to finish the event, was in those vans.

I was careful to align the team members with the level of difficulty in their set of legs. Naturally, I took the hardest legs, the last of which was 11.4 miles through Napa Valley during the hottest time of the day. In less than a day elapsing, in total I ran the most, with more than twenty-seven miles according to my GPS. The second van, our group of six, had a disproportionately higher level of difficulty with our runs as well. Because of this, we had a runner's wife join us that was a personal trainer and certified massage therapist. She helped take the edge off the soreness and provided reminders on nutrition and hydration to prepare us for each leg.

Our IT guy was the last runner on the last leg. Both teams together now, we were cheering him on at different spots those final miles. He was in a world of hurt and it showed. Digging as deep as he could he crossed the finish line. Shortly after he collapsed and refused to let us move him for some time.

The next day, the team was rewarded when we followed the agenda suggested early on by our absent CFO. We walked around Calistoga, had lunch on the scenic patio overlooking vineyards in St. Helena at the Culinary Institute of America, and we went on a couple of wine tours. We reminisced about our trials and tribulations, and how we finished with a more than respectable time considering the collective group's inexperience. We finished the evening at a famous Brewery in Petaluma over a casual dinner.

There were many things I would have done differently on that team building event. The lessons have been learned and the more of these that are conducted, the more polished they become. Those participating developed a tighter bond, but the stories that others in the rest of the company heard pulled non-participants into the experience with us. Funny enough, even some of our customers captured pictures of our decorated vans and blogged about our Ragnar adventure on our owner's group website that was thousands strong. In the end, employees wanted to know when we would have the next company team building event and they wanted to be part of it. The result was silos were brought down and people worked better with each other across departments.

CHAPTER 10

Sales Hiring

| 1 | 2 | 3 | 4 | 5 | 6 | 7 |
| Profile | Description | Sourcing | Screening | Interviewing | Selecting | Onboarding |

S ales hiring is the most influential driver of success[xxiv]. Hiring right yields top revenue growth, encourages efficiency in development, and raises the talent bar. Hiring wrong costs the company money, dilutes development efforts, and lowers the talent bar.

Identifying and executing on the process required to hire right is the crucial initial step. Incorporating onboarding plans incentivized with clear career paths is a comprehensive approach that turns mediocre hiring into world-class sales hiring. This comprehensive hiring process is the way to predictably hire top-performing sales teams.

Start with the unique characteristics of sales hires, which must fit the sales context. What needs to be sold? Thinking of buyer behavior, what attributes are necessary to be successful selling the product or service to the customer? Is the offering highly technical, requiring specialization? Or straightforward with a low level of complexity? What are the points of differentiation for the offering? What experience, skills, education, and personal characteristics of the ideal salesperson are required? Is this role for new business development or to grow existing business? With those questions answered, a candidate profile will emerge.

Time for a thought exercise. A medical device company has a diagnostic machine that is a large capital investment. Similarly, the company has another product—software that optimizes patient care for new systems.

Are these repeat purchases or first-time purchases? Is the sales cycle short and simple, or long and complex? The answer: first-time purchases that have longer sales cycles. That requires sales hires to have knowledge of complex sales cycles *and* consultative sales skills.

Let's do another. A company that makes a consumable product for machines (e.g., mill drills) has specialty store dealers as points of distribution to sell to end customers in metal fabrication crafts. Are these likely repeat purchases or first-time purchases? Long or short sales cycles? This scenario indicates a short sales cycle with repeat purchases. When accounts are making rebuys of the same product or service, sales hires should have negotiation and relationship-building sales skills.

Other considerations involve where the rep will spend the most time. If this is a field sales role, a sales rep with outside sales experience and a realistic expectation of time on the road (e.g., 70 percent travel required) should be included in the job description and the candidate profile. Will the position require that the rep communicate over the phone a significant amount of time? If so, phone skills and call center experience may be important.

The Fluidity of Hiring

Though the hiring process fundamentals remain constant, the candidate requirements change depending on the sales context and the needs of the business.

Recruiting to backfill a fifty-person SDR call center with high turnover is markedly different from recruiting to fill two enterprise account executives several times a year, or even hiring to offset attrition versus hiring to actually increase and grow the headcount of a team.

A person selling a physical product is different than someone selling a service. A SaaS salesperson has to convince someone of a particular service to use by clicking around on a platform, while product sales reps have products that they can demonstrate in hand. The point is that context is key in orientating the sales process fundamentals for successful hiring; sales context, business context, strategic context.

Candidate Profiles and Position Descriptions

Hard to believe as it may be, I've come across many businesses (usually SMB) that have internal job descriptions for everyone in the organization other than salespeople. The more business-oriented firms at least have a sort of candidate profile describing musts and wants.

However, having a consistent position description for reference internally is a fundamental necessity.

Position descriptions vary, though there are some consistent fields that must be included. Allow me to add some color to the following internal position description template:

Job title. Use a job title that accurately conveys the position without inflating the role.

Department. This should be stated as "Sales," though it may also fall into "Marketing." If there are multiple office locations, there should also be a callout here.

Reports To. Insert the job title of the hire's direct supervisor here.

Full-time or part-time. This identifies exempt (salaried with no overtime) or non-exempt (hourly with overtime pay compliant with the Fair Labor Standards Act).

Job Purpose. This section requires a concise description of the job.

Essential Functions. Described in terms of outcomes, the major functional areas should be called out in this section.

Job Goals. A breakdown of overall goals, KPIs to measure each goal, and ranking of importance should be included. A percentage of time to be allocated to those goals can also be assigned in this section.

Resources. List the most important functions in the organization that the hire can rely on as a resource to achieve goals.

Candidate Attributes. Experience and essential job-related skills should belong in this section. Much of what is created in the candidate profile can be imported here.

Here is a sample of a possible Position Description using the described template:

Title:	Account Manager, Texas
Department:	Sales
Reporting to:	Director of Sales, Southwest

Full-Time   ☒   Exempt   Part-Time   ☐   Non-Exempt

Purpose

Be a brand ambassador for the company in assigned territory. Meet/exceed sales objectives of assigned territory by growing existing accounts and bringing on new accounts to grow the territory. Use of professional sales techniques, product service, and development of long-term customer relationships to achieve objectives.

Essential Functions:

- Activities
  - Target accounts based on cost to sell/service, potential revenue, and success potential
  - Increase market share, advise accounts on stocking levels tailored to their buyers, expand selection of offerings and provide product knowledge coaching
  - Respond immediately to requests, participate in shows, update accounts on promotions, and be consistently thorough and knowledgeable about company offerings

- Time Management
  - Call on accounts in proximity of each other to reduce travel time
  - Avoid traveling during peak times of congestion
  - See first account by 8 a.m. and last account by 4 p.m.
- Organization
  - Prepare and plan each sales call utilizing Friday office hours weekly
  - Take detailed notes and handle issues that arise immediately after sales calls
  - Keep demonstration products in mint condition and treat company property as if it was your own
- Administrative
  - Consistently update the sales pipeline using CRM
  - Submit all expense reports before the fifth day of the following month
  - Book necessary travel two weeks in advance

Position Goals

Goals	Measures	Importance
Grow existing accounts	YoY percentage of increase aligned with company objectives.	High
New account acquisition	Number of new accounts and total revenue generated over previous year.	High

Improve customer and prospect engagement	Work three end customer facing shows on average per quarter with $50,000 in closed sales.	High
Communicate marketing initiatives to customers and prospects	Tracked through sales orders received during the promotion period.	High
Increase brand awareness	Monitor customer acquisition to determine effectiveness of sales and marketing efforts.	Medium

Resources

- Director of Sales, Southwest
- Product Managers, Marketing
- Application Specialists, Marketing
- VP of Sales, USA

Attributes

Experience

- Experience with short & long sales cycles
- Experience selling related products and applications
- Top 10 percent field rep at previous company
- Proficient use of CRM

Personal and job-related skills

- Strong communication skills, capable of explaining complex applications or process
- Reliability, consistency in follow-up and accountability
- Sound negotiation and consultative selling skills
- Commitment to providing exceptional service
- Coachable, curious, competitive, disciplined, and has a strong work ethic
- Ability to work independently, with little supervision
- Orientation toward continuous improvement
- Tech stack proficiency

Position descriptions contain soundbites to be used when crafting job descriptions for publication. The initial draft can be created by the hiring manger, but several people in the organization should edit and review it to ensure it accurately conveys the core content of the internal position description. More importantly, the job description should be screened so it doesn't appear to discriminate against anyone.

The Legal Lessons of Job Descriptions

As sales leaders for our own regions, we were given plenty of rope to operate. For the most part that was a good thing. But sometimes too much rope provides enough slack to inadvertently hang oneself. At least that's how it felt when we got in trouble for a job posting.

My counterpart on the other coast posted a sales rep job to fill a position in his region. Before we knew it, we were contacted by the Equal Employment Opportunity Commission (EEOC). The job posting started something like this, "We are looking for a young man . . .."

It could have been much worse, of course. It could have said we are looking for a young Christian male who is a U.S. citizen, straight, white, single, disability free, and with no military experience. We had more than fifty employees at the time, and we were in the EEOC's crosshairs.

We reviewed the description, knew the sales leader well, and understood that it was just a simple oversight, an honest mistake. That didn't matter to the EEOC. They asked for documentation of applicants from all the sales leaders regardless of regions that were hiring for similar positions in different territories. We were subpoenaed, and somehow, we needed to comply, which could dig us deeper.

In uncharted waters, we reached out to our attorneys who painted a very bleak picture of the situation to put it mildly. The impression was that the EEOC had a team of hundreds of lawyers with unlimited resources. They could bury us if they wanted, so it was best to just comply and take our medicine. With our tail between our legs, we did exactly that.

We received a fine so large that several of us had to recount the zeros to verify the amount. Really, most businesses would go under in that same circumstance. We managed to get a reduction, still too incredible of an amount to mention.

What I will say is we had to send checks out to applicants that we disqualified for the position nationally in the sum of tens of thousands of dollars. There was a statute of limitation from when we cut the checks and when they expired, and we were required to honor those amounts even if they were cashed years later. Fortunately for us, most of the checks went uncashed, but a few people received a nice surprise in the mail.

Lesson learned: job descriptions should be drafted to ensure they don't expose the organization to discrimination lawsuits.

Sourcing Talent

I'm a big advocate of hiring when there is no vacancy. It is good insurance to have some potential employees in mind for when the company expands or if a rep departs. The hiring process takes considerable time, and it carries opportunity costs and additional work for existing staff. The longer the position is open, the greater the cost and pressure on staff, which leads to substandard hires to get the position filled. Having a hotlist of potential hires is a great insurance policy.

I invite sales leaders to watch salespeople in the wild. There's no need for a formal interview until ready to pull the trigger to fill the position. Observing potential employees when they're in the throes of selling and don't know they're under consideration for a job is the best way to evaluate prospective sales employees in my opinion. For raw and unfiltered results, sales leaders should be open to those opportunities.

Networking to get warm intros and to connect with candidates is a fruitful avenue for sourcing. Getting introduced through network connections can be timely, particularly if there's news of foreboding times at a prospect's present company and the potential for good salespeople to consider leaving. After being connected, planting seeds that your less-volatile company with growth opportunities is looking for an ideal candidate, can only benefit you. Perhaps your connection isn't interested, though they are willing to put you in touch with interested coworkers or others they know in their network. This approach generates momentum for sourcing solid candidates.

The next avenue to pursue is poaching. There is appropriate and inappropriate poaching. Let me shed some light on the difference with a few real-world examples.

Rob was always a really nice and understanding guy. We got along great, and we respected each other mutually. He was also one of our first B2B customers, and he supported us to the best of his ability given the limitations of his market. His operation wasn't very large, and he did all his purchasing in an open office where other staff members were an earshot from our conversation at all times. After covering the essentials for the sales appointment and securing a new product order, I casually mentioned an open position that our company was desperate to fill and asked Rob if he knew of anyone that could fill that role. His demeanor changed, he asked me to follow him into the warehouse where staff was nowhere to be seen.

He suddenly lunged toward me and said with fury, "Don't *ever* bring up the topic of hiring around my employees again. I'll kick you out of this place for good and never stock another one of your products again! It's hard enough keeping our employees. I don't want them jumping ship to my vendors." I was shocked and felt embarrassed because it was just an innocent ask, but I was too naive to understand the consequences in the moment.

Over a year later, there were some very promising individuals I came across with our channel partners. Since I knew we would be scaling, I monitored their employment situation, though I was careful not to cross any lines overtly after that experience with Rob.

One guy was a go-to person, jack of all trades and a hard worker, exactly what we needed at the time. A purchasing agent said she was going to lose him as soon as a better opportunity came along. This time I took the owner aside privately, prefaced the conversation with what I learned from the purchasing agent, and asked him for his permission to have an initial conversation about possible employment. The owner said he was losing that employee regardless, and he trusted me and the company, so he gave his blessing. It worked out so well that he became one of my best hires for the company. The MacGyver of the organization is still there after fifteen years and became a company pillar.

Oddly enough, some of my best hires were from outside the industry. At the time I was sourcing for the San Francisco Bay Area. After nearly a year, including working with a recruiter that specialized in the territory, I could not find the right person for the role. Again, and again, candidates seemed to have a sales methodology that was not a fit or demanded a king's ransom for the position. I knew I needed someone who could sell premium products, who took initiative, who had a strong work ethic, and who was crafty for the role. I was tipped off by my sister-in-law about a guy working at Salvatore Ferragamo in San Francisco's Union Square. She said that presumably he was their star salesperson and might be interested in making a change.

Acting like a secret shopper, I wanted to see him in action. There were three other salespeople working the store, and at the time there was just two possible customers in the store. The first to greet me and try to earn my business was the rep in question, Franck. Thick French accent, he was on it, taking my shoe size and having me peruse the accessories while he grabbed a few $1,000 pairs of shoes for me to try. Another customer walked in, Franck came out and greeted her, directing her into an area while helping me with my shoes. He asked me to walk around the store for a couple of minutes to test the feel, granting him the chance to engage with the new customer. This continued for another thirty minutes, and he tried to get every customer and every sale. I was impressed with his initiative, tact in working with multiple clients, his work ethic, and ability to sell someone a $200 tie and a $3,000 pair of shoes (no, not me). We ended up hiring him, and he became one of our best salespeople. May be too good. He started dating my sister-in-law, and they eventually married and had two children! He ended up working for the parent company in a different division over twelve years later.

After these experiences, I had greater talent acquisition success and avoided tarnishing relationships with our B2B customers. I would look at the territory, essential skills and other attributes to fit the territory role, then search for salespeople in the wild that fit before approaching their bosses for permission. The hires I ended up securing turned out to be long-term employees and top performers.

Create a Farm System

Becoming an active corporate sponsor of higher education institutions that offer accredited sales certifications and degrees is a form of networking and brand marketing that puts the company in front of a steady stream of qualified candidates to source. While this approach is time intensive, and there are investments to be made upfront, the return down the road is much greater than the investment, though.

Attend career fairs. Sponsor sales competitions. Participate as a guest speaker. Meet with sales professors. All of these activities will help you impart influence, so when graduation nears students that have been formally trained in the art and science of selling are available to fill open positions. These students come with a degree of polish and a sales foundation that is easily built upon to produce superstars for the applicable sales context.

Few companies do this because it takes a concerted effort, investment in time and resources. For those that do, their sourcing headaches are small in comparison.

Traditional Avenues of Sourcing

Internally, the company should have at least a single person dedicated to sourcing talent. Not to be confused with an internal recruiter that just posts jobs, does initial phone screens, sets up interviews, and works a salaried 9-to-5 job. This person should be incentivized through variable pay to bring in qualified candidates for hire across departments (more on incentive pay in a later chapter). This role also monitors job boards and handles incoming applicants from job boards and the company website. Because this sourcing is for the entire company, a robust internal recruiter role is necessary for most growing businesses.

According to the *Jobvite 2019 Recruiting Benchmark Report*[xxv], approximately 50 percent of applicants come from job boards, 35 percent from internal career sites, and less than 1 percent of those who apply through both are offered positions. We can speculate the reasons ranging from active candidates are not as good as passive candidates that are in higher demand, as well as the power of networking and how much more assuring an introduction from a known entity is when considering a candidate. The takeaway is job boards and internal career site candidates are statistically inefficient compared to the other sourcing methods already described.

Still need more sources for ongoing top of funnel screening? You should. Recruiters can be an option. When the company is new to a market, is under time constraints for placement, or needs expertise in candidate screening, hiring a recruitment agency becomes a viable option. Important to note, recruiters have numerous clients and like any smart salesperson, they will prioritize the clients that pay highest, yet they expect the company they work with (you) to stay exclusive with them to prevent duplicate outreach for the same candidate(s). Recruitment firms advocate they are less risky as well because they offer guarantees that take the form of candidate replacement within an agreed upon time should the candidate they recommended and was hired not work out during the probationary period. Speaking from personal experience, the second candidate replacement is less urgent for the agency and the screening less thorough, so best to get it right the first time.

Recruitment agencies are hired based on contingency or retainment. The latter requires an upfront fee to start the search, which can be as high as 50 percent of the first year's salary for the candidate to be hired (e.g. $100,000 salary, $25,000 due at search commencement with $25,000 due upon hire). Retained searches should be used when all other options have been exhausted and the sourcing is for a key position. Contingency is more common, where the agency will ask for 25 percent of the first year's salary due upon hire. This is a less risky option because if there is no hire, there is no cost. It's also a great way to test the recruitment firm to see if they are just providing warm bodies or quality candidates for consideration.

There are a host of other avenues for sourcing. Professional organizations within your industry is one. Another more overlooked avenue is from candidates themselves. The aim of interviews should be to always get something of value out of the conversation. That can be finding out what other companies pay for similar positions, market insights, training initiatives and other things that may be adopted to make your company better. The main thing though is to find out if the timing to seek out other candidates from the same place is ripe, or to find out where the candidate's employer sources their candidates.

The final source is referrals. Customers can be a great resource for referring candidates as discussed previously, though I'm mainly referring to B2C customers where the business relationship is less likely to be impacted. Referrals from suppliers or vendors, also a viable source. Don't forget current employees, they should have people in their network that can be considered. The company should have a referral program where referred candidates from employees equates to a hiring bonus incentive. I like to structure it so each additional referral candidate hired earns 50 percent more for the employee that made the recommendation (e.g. $1,000 for the first candidate, $1,500 for the second, $2,250 for third, and so on). If all these sourcing avenues are still not drumming up candidates, modifying the job requirements is probably necessary, mainly the need for experience.

Hiring Inexperienced Salespeople

Not all sales positions require sales experience, people need to start somewhere. In fact, everyone should work a sales job at some point in their life. Retail store sales experience is most prevalent among those with limited experience. That is a mixed bag because how much selling really occurs in those stores? It varies greatly and, in most cases, positions boil down to order processing, inventory organization, and handling returns. There are other ways to screen for sales aptitude and the characteristics required to be successful in a given sales context.

The scenario is we need to fill ten open SDR positions. These are entry-level positions with entry-level pay. Getting a solid candidate with sales experience is not realistic and not a focus. We turn to our network at the local universities. Based on anecdotal evidence, I've found entrepreneurship majors make the best sales hires for call centers when sourcing for little or no sales experience positions. They are genuinely curious and want to learn how things work. They ask good questions, ticking the curiosity box. Add to that intercollegiate sports backgrounds (competitive), and a demonstrated full schedule of classes while interning or holding a part time job (work ethic), plenty of candidates can be considered. The biggest challenge I've found in hiring straight out of school is ambition. For those rare candidates that fulfill the characteristics and come prepared for the interview, there is usually an offer letter waiting for them. Sales leaders can groom these qualified candidates into successful sales professionals. It begins with an open mind.

Screening for Sales Characteristics

Assuming there is empirical proof that based on the buying context, specific characteristics lead to successful sales hires, the next step is effectively screening for those characteristics. The attributes for the sales position then requires us to look for candidates that are coachable, curious, competitive, and have a strong work ethic. First let's define these characteristics, then we will cover screening recommendations together.

Coachable. Is that a real word? Absolutely! I've been using it for years. It means a person that is capable of receiving coaching. That is taking coaching and then implementing the coaching immediately. This characteristic applies to every sales context I've ever encountered, though it's weighted lighter for transactional selling.

What seems to work well when screening for coachability is running role plays that mirror real life calls. Be forewarned, though, getting candidates on the phone with live customers to see how well they perform is not only unprofessional, it's inaccurate because it isn't in a consistent controlled environment where a valid basis for comparison can be applied. There was a firm I worked for that actually used to screen candidates this way. I made it a priority to modify it to a controlled role play with specific intent.

Here's what to do. After the initial required interview questions (e.g., Tell me about yourself, etc.) Give the candidate some context on the buyer and what is attempting to be sold. Then ask the candidate to influence the prospect (you) in three specific ways. Describe start and stop and then have at the role play. When finished, ask the candidate how they think they did. Good candidates have something of value to offer, they should point out something analytical. That's when you should point out what they did right, and how to improve. Instruct them on two more points for the role play and do the role pay again. Follow the same review process.

Putting it into practice, let's run a hypothetical coachability screening for an SDR position. We are zeroing in on the qualification call with a touch of discovery.

Hiring manager: Bearing in mind that we haven't trained you, we're going to run a couple of role plays. This will give you a taste of a typical function of the job, and give us an impression of your ability. Is that okay?

Candidate: Sure!

Hiring manager: The prospect has requested that a rep reach out to him. He is looking to hire a painter to repaint the house exterior. As is the case so many times, the information filled out by the prospect through our website only contains his name, address, phone number, and project type. Before we can connect him with a painter from our vast database, we must verify that he is indeed the property owner to ensure he has the authority to make changes to the house, we need to verify timeline, when to have the job started or completed, and budget. Do you have all that or should I repeat it?

Candidate: I'm taking notes. I've got it.

Hiring manager: Okay. Here we go. Three, two, one. Hello?

Candidate: Hi, is this Steve?

Hiring manager: It is.

Candidate: Great! I'm calling about the painter request you submitted online. I'm with Widget Co.

Hiring Manager: Right, okay.

Candidate: I'd like to verify some information to get you connected with the right painter for the job. First, are you the property owner or a renter?

Hiring manager: Yes, well, I'm responsible for the mortgage, the bank technically owns the property.

Candidate: Ha-ha. Is there a specific time you had in mind to get work started?

Hiring manager: ASAP. I'd like the work done before Labor Day.

Candidate: Got it. How about budget, what would you be looking to spend for this project?

Hiring manager: No more than $3k.

Candidate: Okay, with that information I will process your request and you should hear from a painter soon.

Hiring manager: Good job. Role plays can be unnerving. How do you think you did?

Candidate: Well overall. I probably could have done better on the budget question. I opened the door for a low-ball response.

Hiring manager: I tend to agree on the budget question. I like how personable you were during the call yet direct and respectful of the customer's time.

Candidate: Thanks.

Hiring manager: Let's do it again, but this time I want you to really get the budget amount to a more realistic figure. There is a technique I want you to use, and it kills two birds with one stone because we need to get project details anyway. In fact, painters screen the jobs we send them for consideration and accept the ones with thorough descriptions 37 percent more of the time. So, collect project details about the paint job and then immediately follow with the budget question, it puts the amount of work required into perspective. Then I want you to suggest you will connect me with the three most-qualified painters that match my preferences based on timeline, budget, and quality. I will push back so be prepared to convince me that it is in my best interest to speak with three of them. Let's assume we already got to timeline. Go ahead and continue the role play when ready.

Candidate: We need details about your project. What work needs to be done?

Sales manager: The house has wood siding with some paint that is peeling, so it probably needs to be prepped properly with sanding.

Candidate: Do boards need to be replaced or any repairs before reapplying paint?

Sales manager: Yes. There is dry rot all over the trim, and a few siding boards need to be replaced as well.

Candidate: What square footage is the home?

Sales manager: About 2,200 square feet.

Candidate: I have a 2,200 square foot home that requires sanding prep and replacement of dry rot trim and siding. For all that work, what do you have budgeted?

Sales manager: I'd like to keep it under $10k.

Candidate: I think we can connect you with three of the painters in your area that are most qualified for the job that match your timeline, budget, and do really good work.

Sales manager: I'd hate to have to meet with three different people, can you just send me your best one, and then I'll decide?

Candidate: We can, but we know that our most satisfied customers are diligent upfront by meeting with at least three because it helps verify scope of work, cost, and personality match. You should feel comfortable with who you hire. Can I set you up with three?

Sales manager: Well, okay.

The main focus is if the candidate actually listened and implemented the coaching. In this scenario, the candidate definitely did and even expanded upon the coaching. Each characteristic should have a rating scale. If I used one to five in this scenario, this candidate might have received a five on coachability.

Screening for curiosity is more subtle. Curious people ask good questions, hence the importance of being curious in sales. It is too easy to become complacent and count any question as a point toward curiosity, don't fall into that trap. They should be really good questions. Good candidates are prepared so questions might go deeper about the company and other than what is already available through public means. Questions that have some nuance regarding the role, the buyer, the product or service, these are all good as long as they are not superficial. "That flagship product you mentioned, do you sell a lot of them?" versus "What percentage of total sales does that flagship product make up in the territory?" Use a point scale to grade the candidate on curiosity.

Screening for competitiveness is done before speaking with the candidate, and after. There is an assumption if the candidate was already a top salesperson, they probably were competitive, that should still be verified. Other indicators include being on collegiate sports teams, academic decathlon, or speech and debate teams. During the interview, I like asking the candidate to provide an example of a time they were competitive. The way they tell the story and how well they sell their competitive nature provides insight into their sales ability as well as screening for competitiveness. Grade the candidate on the point scale depending on the response.

Proving work ethic can be tricky. Asking the candidate to describe their work ethic only has so much credibility. Who is going to say they put in the minimum to get the job done and then check out? Instead it's something like, "I'm the hardest working person I know," or

"Nobody can outwork me." Certainly, they have to be convincing enough to believe they have a strong work ethic. Though this is best verified when checking references. Asking references to rate the candidate's work ethic and explain why they gave that rating lends greater credence.

Of all the candidates, you have narrowed it down to the top two which have similar experience, skills, and similar characteristics scores. Who do you pick? The candidate that adds diversity to the team via different skills, different background, or different experience should have a leg up when it is a stalemate which is seldom.

Hiring Landmines to Avoid

Third rate sales reps are hired by third rate sales managers. The reason is because they hire in their own image. I can think of several instances where I was in a room with a sales manager that was surrounded by reps that looked, acted, and had similar interests to each other. In fact, there is one instance that stands out when I was next to my boss and he saw the same thing except he took it a step further as a small group of sales reps followed their sales manager behind in a single file as they serpentine through the crowded room, "Look at the ducklings following their mother duck."

Sales leaders are mindful not to hire in their own image. Sales leaders hire objectively, based on the needs of the position. It is easy to hire enjoyable people; the primary object is to hire the candidate that is best suited for the job.

The most common complaint of departing salespeople is that they were oversold on the job. That's not to say the hiring manager shouldn't be passionate about the company, the position, and the future. The first sales commandment and cardinal rule number one apply here—do not business develop! The job itself should be described using facts and setting reasonable expectations from the onset.

At a startup I heard a manager tell candidates that he liked that after a few months they could expect to become managers and build out their own teams. That was simply not in the plans and an outright lie, but that manager only cared about getting the hire and the pat on the back from a Founder. Instead he got a verbal slap upside the head by me for breaking cardinal rule number one of sales.

The final landmine to avoid is hiring reactively. Budget limitations, timing, and strategic initiatives influence the ability to bring on new talent. Unless the company is barely surviving and there is a hiring freeze, sales leaders should always be looking. If there is no open position and there is a fantastic and affordable candidate, create a position. Otherwise, sales leaders should build their bullpen.

Candidate Assessment Tools

When used properly, candidate assessment tools increase the chances of making the right hire. They serve as an additional data point and filter out less serious candidates not willing to take the assessment. The proliferation of offerings in this category provides options that meet the unique requirements of candidates for specific sales roles.

Selecting the assessment tool that adequately tests for the qualities required to fit the specific role helps narrow down the field. Customer service-oriented roles commonly use situational judgement tests. Technical skills tests are used for sales engineer roles. For field sales, cognitive ability tests, communication skills tests, and personality assessments may be incorporated with situational judgment tests. Psychometric assessments are becoming popular since they purportedly provide a complete view of candidate stability for the role by testing for attributes including critical reasoning, intelligence, motivation, and personality. Phone screened candidates that are passed on to the next stage typically take the assessment before in-person interviews. Assessments with the right parameters filter through candidates that are a fit.

There are additional considerations when deciding on an assessment tool. Assessment tools should be EEOC compliant—no reason to expose the company to lawsuits from ambulance chasers. They should be customizable to meet the parameters of the role and an acceptable range for candidate inclusion consideration. Lastly, the assessment tool should be scientifically validated.

In experimenting with various assessment tools, speaking with sales leaders in other industries, and getting feedback from HR experts, assessment tools offer quick and dirty results that tick the boxes at a high level. For the more elaborate and time-demanding assessments, provide granular details that are borderline creepy. In speaking with an HR generalist at a Fortune 50 company about the candidate assessment tool they used, she said the assessments took well over two hours and results were so detailed they could determine the brand of toilet paper the candidate used! How much granularity is necessary depends on the defined requirements of the position and what an ideal hire would be. The ideal hire serving as a bullseye with concentric rings going out to the margins of the target as acceptable for further consideration. Good assessment tools offer interview questions for candidates based on their results and potential areas of discrepancy for the role.

My preference was a quick and dirty assessment tool for all our sales hires, later combined with a separate sales methodology specific assessment that provided detail and that required considerably more candidate time. I wanted to make the recruiting process more cost effective, efficient, and easy for candidates early in the hiring process, so I pushed for an assessment tool that took less than five minutes for prospective employees to fill out online.

The Predictive Index® was selected based on its history and the level of details provided with a fast assessment experience for the candidate. The history was intriguing, and I was an instant fan. During WWII, a U.S. Army Air Corps team beat the odds when after flying thirty missions, they didn't suffer a single combat casualty. Psychologists were brought in to study what made their teamwork so successful. The Founder of The Predictive Index® was on that team, and exposure to psychometric testing whet his appetite enough that after the war he attended Harvard, where he studied workplace psychology and in 1952 launched the first Predictive Index Assessment. Over the course of decades, it has been iterated into its effective current form.

We used *The Predictive Index®* for many years as a standard part of the sales hiring process. It disqualified candidates that weren't willing to take the time to fill out the online questionnaire. It filtered out candidates based on a target set with the behavioral and cognitive qualities of top salespeople. It provided advice on the most effective ways to approach employees to help them reach their full potential. I championed its use, but as we dove headfirst into implementation of a new sales methodology, we landed in a shallow pool, there was a need for an additional assessment tool that zeroed in on candidates best suited to perform with that sales methodology.

For the sales methodology assessment, we used an original tool from the SHL Group Ltd. The assessment was conducted as a fourth step, after the phone interview (by a sales leader) and before the candidate was invited to our HQ in the sticks for an in-person panel interview. The short of it is sales professionals fall into five distinct profiles. Through external and internal analytics, we could quantify which profile was most likely to do well with the new sales methodology, and that also matched our top performing salespeople. More importantly, we knew which profiles to stay clear from. For candidates that fell within range and were offered the position, the assessment helped us coach candidates to level up by identifying gaps.

Using assessments provides an objective way to select candidates that are right for the job. The science provides confidence in the decision, and the analytics help sales leaders be more effective in developing team members. With the many options available on the market today, there is surely an assessment tool that fits the unique ideal candidate parameters of any sales role.

Interview Tips for Leadership

The EEOC incident taught me things that made me a better sales leader. Up until that point, offensive jokes from salespeople, discriminatory comments made in jest, were part of the environment which replicated our industry to an extent. None of us said or did anything, we let the reps have open conversations, they were all adults or at least that was our attitude. The EEOC incident taught me that was not acceptable, that leadership is responsible to address company culture that may make people feel discriminated against even if the comments aren't meant to be overtly malicious. The incident taught me to raise the level of professionalism for myself and for the sales force.

That lesson applies to conducting interviews. Highly vetted interview questions that are objective and free of discriminatory implications must be used. Interviewers should follow a methodical process that is nearly identical with every candidate—not only to make it fair for candidates so they are held to the same standard, but to provide a true basis to score interviewees. A standard method encourages process optimization over time. There should be a reference template that has ideal answers to the interview questions so anyone that conducts the interview can objectively and unequivocally grade responses that rank as 10s from those that are 1s. Several people should conduct stages of the interview to gain more data points before a final decision is made.

Interviews should also be done based on how the position will function communication wise. For SDRs that are on the phone, a portion of the interview should be conducted over the phone to vet phone sales skills. Having a methodical, thorough, and objective process that is above board leads to world class sales hiring.

Startups are notorious for allowing sales managers to wing it during interviews. At a startup there was a manager and his direct report interviewing a candidate that was within earshot. What I heard was appalling. This candidate had more experience than the both of them combined, she was an expert in her field, and gracious in how she handled the interview. The leg up the interviewers had was that they went to top tier schools. Probably without realizing it, they were pretentious, chauvinistic, and arrogant. They completely winged it, asking random questions that had no value, akin to conversation keepers a stranger might ask at a party. That is, they asked questions that were often times rhetorical, hogging the interview time by speaking much more than the candidate.

Additionally, when open positions required that several department heads interview candidates, the directive from a Founder was not to share notes or coordinate our interview questions so we can form our own opinions. When candidates are asked the same questions by different people, the impression is leadership doesn't know what they are doing. When the interview process is disjointed, inconsistent, and interviewers have free reign on the questions they will ask, the company is greatly exposed to discrimination lawsuits and will make hires based subjectively on likability rather than objective fit for the role. That startup had just crested fifty employees. An EEOC audit could have ripped them apart.

Onboarding

After painstaking analysis to create a solid position description, and the interview vetting process, offer letters have been sent out and accepted. Now what? Part of the hiring process is getting new hires up to speed. The onus is on the company to invest in training and resources to bring the candidate to standard as soon as possible and on a trajectory to reach full potential from the start. The onboarding process should be regimented with transparent milestones that have to be met. Over time the onboarding process requires iteration for optimization and adjustments based on the stage of the company, any pivots that have been made that have changed the sales process, and adjustments to the position requirements.

Though the hires are vetted for fit, direct supervisors should identify skill gaps, prior to and during the first phase of onboarding. A best practice is to have a survey sent out to a half dozen references with leadership responsibility in order to identify new hire gaps in advance of the first day of employment. This can be produced on a shoestring budget by software engineers on hand or more professionally through a company like *SkillSurvey Inc.* that provides a background check option that can be integrated digitally into the hiring and onboarding process. The objective is to have a supplemental development plan prepared prior to employee arrival.

The new hire should also have some skin in the game with preliminary preparation. Companies have their own vernacular, and for new hires, just speaking the same language becomes a challenge in the beginning. There are acronyms specific to the business, enterprise vocabulary, industry specific terms, backend system references, and the list goes on. Sales leaders should provide new hires with a list of commonly used words and encourage new hires to familiarize themselves with that list in order to reduce anxiety during onboarding and to accelerate retention. It is also a prudent first test since hires that come prepared having studied the list of terms are a good sign.

Coordination is an important component of the onboarding process. This starts with strategically assigning a start date that leverages resources. Will everyone that needs to be part of the onboarding be available during that time period? Are their schedules locked for the commitment? If there are multiple hires for the same or similar positions, they should be grouped to go through the training together. Even in cases when the roles are separate, the initial company orientation, training on systems and tech stack, can be done together for efficiency.

Milestones were mentioned earlier. New hires should be told on their first day about milestones and what to expect. They will be drinking out of a firehose for the first few weeks, but they should be reassured that the training curriculum is designed to start foundationally and become more advanced to ensure the content sticks. To keep true to that promise, I like designing curriculum into modules: beginner, intermediate, and advanced.

Each training module has a theme and purpose. The beginner module introduces the new hire to the marketing framework for proper company orientation. They are put through the buyer's journey to experience the typical buying process and gain an appreciation for the buyer's challenges. They are trained on the basics of the business such as the sales org makeup, key terms, and what the systems are used for in the tech stack. The intermediate module goes into the use of backend tool process, systems, and sales process. The advanced module doubles down on the previous module with nuance to be tested. New hires are shadowed during the intermediate and advanced modules, encouraged to learn through doing and to fail early and often, so smaller value deals are provided that are less financially risky for the company. As new hires become more proficient, they are given more autonomy yet adhere to the general onboarding process.

Each module has a test at the end that must be passed with a score of 80 percent or higher, or else the candidate has to be rolled back to repeat parts that were missed in the module. If the candidate cannot retain the content or pass the same module a second time, they must be cut loose. This is rare but it does happen. If the candidate is allowed to slide there is a good chance the inevitable will be delayed and they will eventually be terminated before the end of training or within a year of employment. Having a hard and fast rule also motivates those doing the training to do their duty to the best of their ability and discourages complacency. Everyone going through the process should be held to the same standard. Being vigilant through the process and holding everyone to high standards produces the best trained hires.

There are indicators that the onboarding plan is getting better or getting worse. The strongest indication that the onboarding plan is getting better is when new hires who are trained up keep raising the performance bar. We saw that at a technology company where our new hires were outperforming our veterans in short order. Raising the bar forced existing team members to step up or self-select and step out. When the onboarding plan is not working the way it is intended, it will present itself in replicative coaching, struggling performance, and complaints from coworkers about the new hire. It is the responsibility of sales leadership to have an iterative onboarding process that is effective.

Career Path

I'm a big advocate of transparency. If I were in an entry-level sales position, I would want to know what the next career step was and how to get there. I would also want to know how far I could go with all things being equal and realistic. Salespeople should be granted this transparency their first day, even during the interview process when a candidate asks about career trajectory. It should be backed with data to indicate what is possible and a realistic timeframe. Sticking to the facts and avoiding overselling is paramount.

Sales leaders who are new to the organization have to inherit existing staff and must adapt to legacy issues. I am no stranger to this predicament, it is expected. After restructuring the call center into specific teams based on assessed skills, capabilities, and potential, I created a formal process for career advancement. In a Silicon Valley technology startup formality isn't exactly accepted, but some things require adherent organizational structure and the path to career advancement falls into that category. The career path for call center employees ended up looking similar to this:

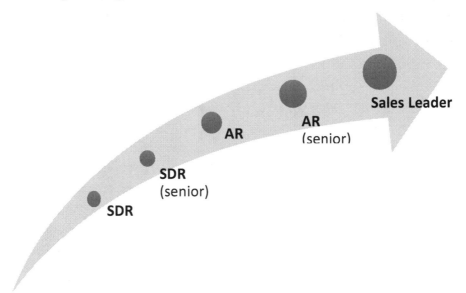

Back to transparency: employees should know what each position pays. This is a controversial topic. Many companies I've come across expect employees to keep their compensation private. That's a nice thought, but it's unrealistic because people talk and ultimately upper management gets bit.

There was a territory sales rep who had a solid territory but substandard performance. Other territories were growing significantly faster, and territory redesign was on the agenda. We were splitting a nearby territory, and it made the most geographic sense to incorporate part of this rep's territory—that meant the cost to keep that employee versus what he brought in, which was already at close to break even, didn't justify keeping him. He wasn't bringing in new accounts, and even to do so, it would take years before breakeven was reached. Add to that he was simply not a fit for our company culture and I could no longer allow his direct supervisor to protect him. I had to personally notify him of his termination.

This rep was contentious with many of our reps, one in particular who worked a territory hundreds of miles in the same region—David, for reference. David had a tendency to be condescending to Phil. During sales meetings, Phil might repeat something obvious the product manager had said, and then David would say in a condescending tone, "Yes, good Phil."

Well, when Phil was hired, he came from the industry and brought with him experience that his sales leader valued, so he was given higher compensation than David who came from another industry. When Phil's employment was terminated, he sent David a copy of his annual pay. Livid, as to be expected, David confronted their sales leader who hired them both, and asked why Phil made more money when Phil's territory did substantially less than David's. Responding in what can be described as the wrong answer, David was told that Phil was a better negotiator than him! David proceeded to share Phil's pay with other reps across the region and that created a firestorm that we had to put out.

Good things came out of that dramatic chain of events. Aside from David moving on to another company of his own accord, my pleas to standardize pay for the position were finally considered. The transparency addressed the rumor mill and freed us from distractions to keep us focused on our jobs. Salespeople returned to their motivated state void of the previous distractions.

Having learned from the Phil and David incident, later on in my career, I was sure to work with my sales leaders in the call center at that technology company to establish pay standards for each position. We created a base salary consistent with each team along with variable pay tiers that were specific to team's results. Everyone on the team knew what bonus would be paid out for the top performer and had a personal dashboard linked to how they were tracking on variable pay. Before long we had consistency and transparency in pay.

I was not out of the woods yet. There was only tenuous support from a company Founder. The biggest bone of contention he raised was that the company (him) reserved the right to hire people with more experience and place them on higher paying teams, even making exceptions to pay them more than existing staff on the same team. Doing so would open the candidate pool to top talent from his perspective. That approach was understandable to an extent.

However, it discredited the entire sales organizational structure put in place, and made the sales leaders appear to be disingenuous about the career path they outlined since outsiders could leapfrog the process and block out existing staff from filling promotion slots. It undermined the efforts of the staff who were striving for career advancement. Furthermore, experienced sales reps who were successful at other companies under different sales contexts were no guarantee they would be superstars. In fact, they were unlikely to be as good as our fully trained sales reps who had specific experience and developed skills in our unique sales context.

We had a cost-effective, predictable, repeatable process that was retaining and developing talent to a high caliber. My arguments kept him at bay for a while until a strategic pivot uprooted everything. The most talented reps jumped ship, sales leaders left, and everyone else that stuck it out was eventually let go. In the end, it is the Founder's company, we all received our marching orders from him. Perhaps I'm not as good a salesperson as I used to be or else, he may have been convinced to stay the course and that company would be in a better place.

At the risk of sounding dogmatic, there are other considerations for implementing pay grades. Going back to the distraction of lawsuits, transparent pay reduces claims of discrimination. It helps calibrate appropriate costs for the positions. Pay transparency curtails new hire compensation negotiations, which can derail the hiring process. Instead of candidates trying to negotiate for the highest pay they can get, candidates are compensated on what the position pays at the company—there is no haggling on pay. It really streamlines those discussions, and for the sales members that claim they are God's gift, the variable component rewards top performers with earning potential for their efforts. Their background, skills, and experience got them the job; their performance and not their negotiation skills, will determine how much more they will gain financially.

CHAPTER 11

Compensation Incentive Plans

Hardly any topic is as polarizing as pay. There were times in the workplace when I would have gladly rather talked about religion or politics. That goes to show you how touchy the subject of compensation can get. I've witnessed normally calm and collected people flip out over small discrepancies in pay. While doing a ride-along, at the mere suggestion of changing compensation plans, I even had a field rep slam on his brakes while on the highway and proceed to describe upper management in slang terms I'd heard for the first time, all while we were in harm's way!

Compensation, and in particular, variable pay, is an ultra-sensitive topic. Harnessing that sensitivity to reward the right behavior and drive earnings growth is what I hope will be the takeaway for this chapter.

Given its sensitivity, it's natural to shy away from the topic. That would be a mistake of course and a missed opportunity. Savvy sales leaders use the topic of variable pay to level up their sales organizations.

While doing interviews, I used a filter to great effect when gauging comfort of pay structure. Learning the hard way early on, sales hires demanding base pay to be more than 75% never yielded anything higher than a mediocre performer. In fact, a couple of low performers come to mind. They were adamant about a high base pay structure, and ultimately, we had to let them go. My takeaway: when a rep candidate is adamant about a pay structure dominated by base pay, run the other way!

Pay transparency certainly solves that off the bat, though candidates may assume they can still negotiate the pay structure. Candidates don't know how realistic goal achievement is. Hiring managers should put them at ease by providing proof of what percentage of reps hit target and furnish total gross payment amounts of a given time period as evidence. Assuming accounts or customers already exist, it may make sense to show how the territory is performing without a rep. They should encourage candidates to call several reps to get their overall opinion on how realistic variable pay achievement is.

During ramp up, the company can guarantee a portion of the variable pay or create a draw program where the company pays the target commissions the rep would have earned if up to speed, later to be deducted from future commissions, similar to paying back a loan with no interest. The benefit is the rep transitions into the role with little personal financial disruption. Candidates adept at negotiation may ask for nonrecoverable draws, which means draw commissions paid aren't treated like debt that needs to be offset by commissions. In my opinion, this only makes sense during the training period. After that, a recoverable draw schedule can be put in place for the first year of employment. Draws are usually reserved for reps that come with experience and carry a large quota.

Draw Example

Commission draw is $4,500 a month. In month one, the rep's territory brings in $2,000 in commissions. In month two, the rep's territory brings in $2,800. In month three, the rep's territory brings in $3,500. Over three months the rep has been paid $13,500 ($4,500 x 3) in draw commissions. The rep has earned only $8,300 in commissions. If during ramp up the draw is nonrecoverable, the rep begins month four from $0 owed in commissions and isn't required to pay back the discrepancy amount of $5,200 ($13,500 - $8,300). If the draw is recoverable, the rep will need to bring in over target earnings (in excess of $4,500) for as long as it takes to pay back the $5,200 discrepancy.

The candidate has been informed about the draw schedule, has been shown proof of variable pay achievement with other reps, and has been given references to verify how realistic goals set by the company really are. Yet, if there remains insistence on a higher portion of base pay than variable, then it's time to cut bait!

It may not be necessary to get to that point or into that situation, however. Ask questions during screening such as, "How do you feel about commission versus salary?", and, "Would you prefer a lower salary with uncapped over target earnings (OTE) where you can make more than executives, or do you prefer a higher salary relative to variable pay with much smaller upside?" Those who answer they prefer the higher variable option should remain in the running while those averse to pay for performance should be disqualified from consideration.

I've also discovered that reps who come from a high salary to variable pay structure are much less hungry, have larger expense claims, and work less hours. My best reps came from a strong commission background. Sales rep jobs with the highest-earning potential have a disproportionate amount of pay coming from the variable component, according to the U.S. Bureau of Labor Statistics.

Good reps who want to get out of the variable pay grind and into more stability as they move through life get into sales leadership. The functions of the job in sales leadership are fairly routine, with little day-to-day direct deal closes. As such, they warrant higher salary to variable in most instances. Variable pay should definitely be part of the compensation makeup, and it should be tied directly into the sales team and the company sales goals, where the sales leader has influence.

Incentive Pay Philosophy

There are plenty of people who philosophically disagree with incentive pay. Think of an aquatic park. A place where seals, dolphins, and orcas are rewarded with fish when they perform. That's the analogy used to describe pay for performance. It's not the most flattering comparison, is it? People say they don't want to be manipulated. Those who strongly feel that way should stay out of sales and remain in a routine job where they will be comfortable.

Salespeople have to accept that variable pay will always be a component of their compensation structure. Rather than reject it philosophically, embrace it with a positive attitude. Some of the best salespeople I've come across get charged with the thrill of uncapped earnings. The perspective of many of us is those salespeople who outperform others, that is, those who bust their tails more, have better results, and make more sacrifices to perform at their best, should be compensated more.

The truth is complacent sales organizations lose their best salespeople because they don't reward them commensurate to their performance, but rather cap pay to the lowest common denominator, in effect rewarding mediocre performers identically to top performers. Naturally that discourages salespeople from going above and beyond, and encourages high-caliber sales professionals to seek out positions where there is an opportunity for greater earning potential.

If sale reps are proud, sales leaders are prouder. While pride can be a good characteristic that motivates sales professionals to do more, it can be an Achilles heel as well. For the purposes of this topic, pride can blind sales leaders to financially limit superstars, which in turn hinders talent retainment and discourages new talent.

Sales leaders should be open to the possibility that their direct reports will earn more than them! That's a nonstarter for many in management positions. Pride aside, what's best for the company? In reality, sales leaders make more in the long run while the sales team bar is raised and the company meets growth objectives with a motivated sales staff. So, what's the problem?

Call Center Incentive Plans

Call centers in particular have a significant degree of gamification built into their backend tools. Commonly referred to as their secret sauce, successful sales leaders iterate on creating the most optimized incentive system to maximize call center rep output. Though signed NDAs and hand-shake promises of sharing secret sauces for specific companies prevent me from providing actual call center incentive system recipes, I'm certainly permitted to share common ingredients!

Getting the most output from sales reps is a favorite topic at call centers, so let's start there. Designing an incentive pay structure that motivates reps to work extra hours and attack the phones when they do is the panacea for sales leaders heading up call centers. Driving behavior that increases revenue and motivates reps to go above and beyond is the ultimate objective.

That's the general sauce. Now for the ingredients.

First ingredient: instant gratification. Pay commissions early. During completion of the pay period, reps who get paid what they earned receive instant gratification for their efforts.

Second ingredient: set a base that meets threshold for basic living expenses, considering that the rep will earn some commissions organically with little effort. A base that is too low will attract reps who either don't need the money or won't be hired elsewhere for good reason. Setting a reasonable base will attract the type of reps needed, and drive reps to grind in order to earn more money.

Third ingredient: classes. No, we're not talking back to school. Classes as in segmented groups based on performance. Their commissions are locked for a specific amount of time, and they are guaranteed to start off the next pay cycle in that category. The leaderboard is a critical piece, not only ranking performance in a given period, but also tracking group performance with color-coded callouts. Acknowledging superstars and identifying reps that need to step up is a tactic that encourages competitive reps to work harder to maintain their group status or climb to the higher group. The employee's dashboard, in addition to visuals on activities, objectives, and results, should include a record metric that conveys with an image what the best pay period was for the rep and how far from that performance bar the rep is tracking. Additional commissions should kick in each time the bar is surpassed. Lastly, overt prize assignments for the sales superstar over a specified period provides additional motivation.

Putting It All Together

On the hypothetical screen of a rep is the backend page for tracking customer calls, account info, etc. On the margins is a leaderboard that tracks performance in real time.

This rep is in the top 75 percent of sellers, her name is highlighted in green. Listed below are reps from her team. Reps above 50 percent are yellow, and reps above 25 percent are orange. Those below 25 percent are in red.

She's earning 10 percent of revenue for each booking because she's in the top tier. When she reaches her performance bar and sets a new personal record during the pay period, she will earn an additional 5 percent commission on revenue going back to the first dollar of revenue generated during the pay period.

Money aside, she's motivated to be the superstar in this pay period because the reigning champ, as a benefit for being a top performer, selects preferred office lunch, and there is only so much of the same food everyone except the reigning champ can take. At the end of the quarter, the top salesperson is given a trophy that is displayed above her desk for the following quarter as well.

So, what should you expect when the right balance of ingredients described above produce a delicious sales sauce?

Here's what. Reps work into the nights and willingly come in on weekends. They take only necessary breaks for meals and bathroom visits. Reps optimize their own processes because they are striving to beat their own record and to be in the top class. The rep's pay is commensurate to output, rewarding the rep for the effort and benefitting the company for the revenue captured at an accelerated rate.

Gamification works both ways. Sales leaders need to craft an incentive system that rewards reps that also mitigates financial exposure and bad behavior. What can go wrong? Reps may be rewarded handsomely for doing things that capture little value and drive counterproductive behavior. For instance, in order to get credit for closing the sales cycle or answering the most calls, reps may make halfhearted attempts to lead the field in activity while bypassing valuable results for the company.

Reps game the system with shortcuts. This can have adverse effects on process and procedure, with downstream consequences if they aren't addressed early. For example, certain talking points may need to be strictly adhered to by reps to reduce potential liability or get them to stick to an already optimized script. Reps may curtail that portion of the process for more volume in order to reach quota. To discourage that behavior, there should be checks and balances in place. Transcribed calls can be audited, and reps should receive demerits that count against their earned commissions when they go off script. The compensation incentive system is the framework and may remain in its form through stages of the business. However, compensation incentive plans are iterative. They must be assimilated to the changing conditions of the business. Iterations can be as frequent as the same quarter, depending on business conditions. Agility is merited and changes in plans are more readily accepted when the overall compensation incentive framework remains consistent.

Early-stage businesses may require top-of-line growth to establish a customer base. In that case, the compensation incentive plan should reward reps who bring in the most top of funnel business. As the business environment demands long-term revenue predictability, the compensation incentive plan should be altered to steer business in that direction. Clawback provisions are a stop gap measure between new customer acquisition and greater customer lifetime value. Simply put, reps who bring in new customers are compensated at the determined rate, but if the customer churns before a reasonable amount of time, the value associated with that customer must be subtracted (clawed back) from the compensation for that period.

Field Sales Incentive Plans

We had a field sales rep who was the undisputed leader in signing on new accounts. The next closest rep paled in comparison. On the surface, the rep was a superstar.

Sales leadership did a deep dive and found that after the opening order from that rep, accounts stagnated. Worse, over the course of two years, roughly one-third of accounts self-selected and terminated the business relationship, returning unsold inventory, much of which was obsolete or not resalable. Large inventory returns were disruptive to our warehouse and particularly disruptive with forecasts and supply chain management. When factoring in double handling costs, administration costs, and other overhead associated with each account from that rep, the math made it abundantly clear that the rep's territory was costing the company more than any other territory in the country, yet until that point sales leaders were praising the rep and paying him additional commission dollars for being an avid hunter.

We continued to honor our stock return guarantee with B2B customers much to the chagrin of our finance department and warehouse. To address large returns, we instituted reactionary processes where reps could sell through account inventory. Simultaneously, returned products were counted against the reps who sold them initially by a multiple greater than they were sold initially. In short order reps were selectively opening new accounts with much lower churn and steady growth.

Field sales is another animal. The compensation incentive system is simpler here by default. To make sense of the costs associated with field sales, sales cycles are longer and more complex, so paying commissions early doesn't have the gratification impact it does with inside sales. The fact that sales are typically less transactional leads to more variables and less predictability, mandating compensation plans that keep the reps' feet on the gas throughout the year, including when they've had seemingly irrecoverable quarters.

To achieve that end, I've had success working with finance in designing compensation incentive plans that keep reps focused on quarterly targets with the option to offset soft quarters with a cumulative goal pay out. There's a myriad of ways to structure the plan, given those parameters. Compensation incentive plans work best when they follow the ABCs: *aligned* with the organization's revenue goal, *built* on realistic assumptions, and *constituting* the right behaviors.

Based on history, seasonality, new product releases, and promotions, each territory is assigned a sales target. If the goal is simply to grow the business 20 percent through new account acquisition or expanding existing business, then assign each quarter targets and each territory sales goals that factor into that growth objective. In the following mockup, a rep is given sales targets with quarterly payout objectives plus two tier commissions for OTE where the second-tier acts as a *kicker* (additional payout over threshold). Reps that have a soft Q3 should still hit the cumulative goal and will therefore be paid the difference after year end, though that is not reflected in the below model.

Remuneration Model					Eligible Amount	1% Commission	2% Commission	OTE
	Target	Cumulative	Actual	Cumulative				
First Qtr	$2,500,000	$2,500,000	$3,625,000	$3,625,000	$1,125,000.00	$250,000.00	$875,000.00	$20,000.00
Second Qtr	$3,250,000	$5,750,000	$4,250,000	$7,875,000	$1,000,000.00	$325,000.00	$675,000.00	$16,750.00
Third Qtr	$2,925,000	$8,675,000	$2,415,000	$10,290,000	-$510,000.00	$0.00	$0.00	$0.00
Fourth Qtr	$1,325,000	$10,000,000	$2,645,678	$12,935,678	$1,320,678.00	$132,500.00	$1,188,178.00	$25,088.56
	$10,000,000		$12,935,678					$61,838.56

Tiered commission structures for field sales reps have advantages over flat commissions. Tiered plans are based on milestones to get reps to hit quota, exceed target, and continue growing the business to maximize financial rewards. Financial reward is a form of acknowledgement. Reps who hit the top tier are acknowledged as top performers and paid for their results.

Financial acknowledgments pertain to compensation incentive plans for sales leaders. The variable component should be shared with what sales leaders have a direct impact on and what they contribute to. For example, a variable model comprised of 75 percent direct goal achievement and 25 percent collective goal achievement. Regional top line sales, quotas for growing core products, and new account acquisition can make up the 75 percent portion. A simpler, more conforming model is to have a flat increase in territory growth, giving the sales leader autonomy on what to focus on to get there. Collective goals might include top line company sales, return on sales (*ROS*), and new customer acquisition/retention. Though impacted secondarily, collective goals promote collaboration across functions and encourage sales leaders to have a more holistic view of the organization.

In the following sales leadership incentive plan mockup, four quadrants include individual targets and collective targets.

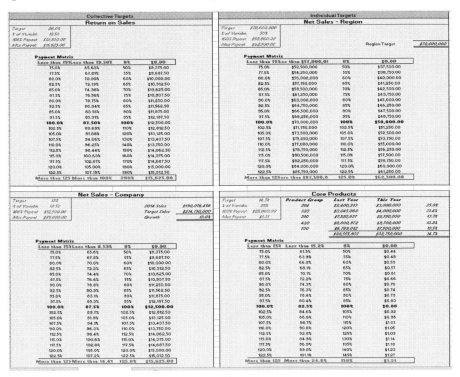

As with the other variable portions in the model, there is capped OTE potential. Capping the variable at the sales leadership level is a byproduct of having a larger base salary, a tradeoff that sales leaders generally accept. There are hybrids to this model that allow a portion of the variable, such as regional sales, to remain uncapped if that's in alignment with the company objectives. For sales leaders with teams who crush goals and exceed max payout, exceptions to capping may be made, especially if the broader company hits revenue targets.

Individual Targets					
Net Sales - Region					
Target	$70,000,000				
% of Variable	50%				
100% Payout	$50,000.00				
Max Payout	$62,500.00			Region Target	$70,000,000
Payment Matrix					
Less than 75%	Less than $57,000,000	0%	$0.00		
75.0%	$52,500,000	50%	$37,500.00		
77.5%	$54,250,000	55%	$38,750.00		
80.0%	$56,000,000	60%	$40,000.00		
82.5%	$57,750,000	65%	$41,250.00		
85.0%	$59,500,000	70%	$42,500.00		
87.5%	$61,250,000	75%	$43,750.00		
90.0%	$63,000,000	80%	$45,000.00		
92.5%	$64,750,000	85%	$46,250.00		
95.0%	$66,500,000	90%	$47,500.00		
97.5%	$68,250,000	95%	$48,750.00		
100.0%	$70,000,000	100%	$50,000.00		
102.5%	$71,750,000	102.5%	$51,250.00		
105.0%	$73,500,000	105.0%	$52,500.00		
107.5%	$75,250,000	107.5%	$53,750.00		
110.0%	$77,000,000	110.0%	$55,000.00		
112.5%	$78,750,000	112.5%	$56,250.00		
115.0%	$80,500,000	115.0%	$57,500.00		
117.5%	$82,250,000	117.5%	$58,750.00		
120.0%	$84,000,000	120.0%	$60,000.00		
122.5%	$85,750,000	122.5%	$61,250.00		
More than 125%	More than $87,500,000	125.0%	$62,500.00		

The regional goal can be designed similar to the rep quarterly targets with a commission kicker to encourage the sales leader to stay aligned with the remuneration models in the same region. Cumulative goal attainment can also be part of this quadrant to keep the sales leader motivated and offset missed targets.

Internal Recruiter Incentive Plans

In the sales hiring chapter, I alluded to adjusting compensation for internal recruiters to have incentive plans similar to those of sales professionals. Dashboards and KPIs may keep internal recruiters focused on the top of funnel tasks to source candidates, while results should be rewarded through the compensation plan. The largest benefit to having dedicated internal personnel for hiring is the time saved providing quality hires for consideration.

Compensation incentive plans must be drawn with the goal of providing quality candidates at the core. Filling positions should be rewarded, as should sourcing the cream of the crop. Again, to encourage the right kinds of behavior, a clawback provision must be included, where sourced candidates who are let go during the first year, or an agreed upon specific time, will be counted against goal.

Compensation Incentive Plan Rollout Protocol

What are the three guarantees in life? Death, taxes, and that compensation plans will change. They really have to in order to adhere to the ever-changing phase of the business and the demands of the buying environment. It's not a matter of *if,* but rather *when* and *how often.* Small tweaks to compensation incentive plans require sensitivity and should be handled with care. Major changes to comp plan framework are the stuff that keeps sales professionals up at night.

Gloom and doom or elation and celebration? Despite the best of intentions, many compensation incentive plan rollouts that have major changes to the comp models fall into that first category. Sales leaders must bring their "A" game and be strategic with their approach. Then comes time to sell like hell.

Given the topic sensitivity, methodical planning is required. Sales leaders and finance teams should have a general idea of the new incentive plan framework to start with. They should agree on a rollout date that provides a clean start, such as the first day of the next fiscal year.

At this point the clock is ticking. Sales leaders need to get the most influential salespeople on their team involved. The success of having direct sales leaders speak to key team members varies depending on the strength of the team leaders' relationships. The best incentive plan iterations I've been involved with were germinated from salespeople feedback. There should be a tight timeframe to collect the responses, which is preferably handled face to face given the topic. Answers and reactions should be presented to the head of sales and involve all sales leaders to gauge consensus.

Get the rest of the sales force involved, too. There are no secrets here. Salespeople talk, and the absence of information inevitably means salespeople will fill in the blanks with skepticism about the new comp model. Excluding the sales force from providing input makes the plan top down, which will put salespeople on the defensive when it's time for launch. Consider providing a carefully crafted, anonymous and optional short survey to the entire sales force on the topic of compensation plan improvements. It's a great way to set a collaborative tone and provides essential feedback for reference later. The survey also orientates sales leadership on model design and gauges rollout timing.

The next step is to build out the value proposition for the new plan. Identify the benefits, such as the increased upside for performance and the possibility for much greater earning's potential compared to the existing plan. Show reps who apply the new comp plan with last year's numbers. This will highlight how much more the rep would have earned if the new plan were in place. Hammer home that the plan is designed to encourage a best-in-class, high-performance sales culture and underscoring that feedback from the sales force helped shape it.

Then comes the selling, which should be done one-on-one and in person in my opinion. Well in advance of the official launch, framework rollout should be presented by the sales leader to individual team members. Remember to tailor the presentation to the individual learning styles of the team. Salespeople tend to be kinesthetic learners, best learning through hands-on methods. Walking through different payout scenarios together using an interactive payout calculator for simulations is effective for this group of learners. Visual learners will retain and understand information better if you use one-page summaries and slide presentations with graphs and charts. For auditory learners, supplement explanations of the comp plan with a recording. The point is sales leaders must be prescriptive with team members, just as they would be with top clients.

At the national sales meeting, the head of sales presents the new compensation incentive plan. This is where survey statistics based on salesperson responses are shared, culminating in the redesigned model. Using a fact-driven approach in this manner garners the support and buy-in of the sales force as well. With the backing of upper management, the change becomes real and imminent.

The final step is getting commitment. Sales leaders go back to their teams for individual sign off. Salespeople are presented with their actual targets for the year and offered the option for a specified amount of time to either stick with the current plan or go with the new model. For significant revisions to the compensation plan (e.g., going from a higher base to a higher variable and lower base) offering the option of a year to transition may prevent flight risks. Top performers will tend to take the new plan immediately because they will likely benefit more. Struggling salespeople will see the writing on the wall and probably leave the company. In the midterm, the entire sales force will transition to the new comp plan. Inevitably reps who benefit from the new design will be vocal and influence others, while those who are struggling will tend to stay quiet to avoid drawing attention to their subpar performance.

When done right, the new compensation plan will have unified support. Mostly unified, I should add. People hate change, especially salespeople. The strongest plan with the best rollout won't convince everyone. Once there's proof, though, performing reps will fall into the elation and celebration bucket. That will influence others to check their skepticism and join rank. A minority of salespeople will remain skeptical no matter what is done, but these laggards will likely accept the change over time when they no longer have a choice.

Landmines to Avoid

Throughout this chapter, best practices were conveyed and suggestions for designing effective incentive plans and rolling them out were provided. Just as there are a myriad of ways to create compensation incentive plans, there are also a myriad of ways to take the most well-designed compensation incentive system and turn it on its head. Let's do everything we can to avoid catastrophe with your new plan. Here are six landmines to avoid:

1) *Mixing sales role responsibilities and accounts receivables role responsibilities.* Sales reps should not function in a collection's role. The moment that happens, the client relationship changes. Finance and sales should certainly communicate to prevent sales reps from wasting time calling on customers who aren't in good financial standing with the company. Reps should be able to guide accounts on extending credit or inform

accounts when they may be reaching credit limits. The line is drawn when it comes to reps exerting pressure to collect on overdue balances, though. That activity should be reserved for accounts receivables/collections.

2) If a degree is required to interpret variable pay, you failed! *Keep it simple* enough for a ten-year old to understand, or thousands of sales reps with different backgrounds all over the planet.

3) *Variable pay delays are a big no-no!* Sales professionals should receive the variable pay achieved as soon as possible. At the end of the pay period. At the end of the month. At the end of the quarter. Or at the end of the year, shortly after they hit the particular target assigned. Sales leaders should hold the finance department accountable (pun intended) to issuing payment immediately. Just as silence begets rumors, delays in pay will impact the trust between the sales professional and the company.

4) *Changing variable pay midway through the fiscal year leads to flight risk.* New variable pay should be rolled out with the least amount of disruption and certainly never midstream through a month or quarter.

5) *Goals that are unachievable have the inverse effect on incentivizing staff.* Sales leaders cannot expect salespeople to take them seriously when they rollout pie-in-the-sky targets that few, if anyone, can hit.

6) *Refusing to pay salespeople their commissions when they are less than 1 percent away from goal.* When salespeople clearly make an effort but still fall a hair short of sales goals it's best to pay part of the variable. Common decency dictates that a concession should be made. Paying at least a portion of the commission satisfies everyone and retains trust. Besides,

there's no such thing as a 100 percent, perfectly projected incentive plan. If that ever happens, perhaps there's a leg to stand on for drawing a hard line.

I personally tripped landmines two through six during my tenure as head of sales for a tech startup. During compensation negotiations I opted for a lower base with higher OTE upside. The variable plan that was proposed to me required a fair amount of deciphering (landmine two). Given my experience in compensation design and my education, I was surprised that it was still a challenge to interpret. I chalked it up to my inexperience in the industry. I assumed it was standard and chose not to make waves as a new hire in a pivotal role.

I was taking a major haircut in base pay to accept the position, so I needed to know how to interpret the compensation incentive plan so I could have an idea where to aim to hit target. Understanding the plan took a detailed translation from the person in charge of operations. He reassured me that targets were achievable and oversold how realistic it would be to achieve them. About two months later he left the company, and I found out shortly thereafter that the targets were overinflated, as was his sales pitch (landmine five). As the first head of sales for the company without a basis for comparison, I had to trust the hiring manager and the Founders. I found myself subsidizing the company by taking a personal financial loss for over six months. Strike one!

Appointments were made with a Founder. Appointments were missed. After a series of false starts and some time working with the person charged with financial models, we eventually settled on a compensation plan. That is after I drew up my own, and we modified it to something mutually agreeable that no longer resembled what I'd drawn up. The first quarter was nearly over by the time it was finalized. With a gauge on what was achievable, it was much more realistic than the first comp plan at least, and I went after my goals with full force. By the end of Q2, I was overachieving on targets and hitting kickers, making up for lost time. There were significant delays in getting my earned variable pay, though, so I had to meet with a Founder again (landmine three).

The end of Q3 rolled around, and I was going to have another record quarter. Then I found out that while my targets remained the same, unknown to me certain sales numbers didn't count (landmine four). Partway through the quarter we rolled out a new sales motion that involved sharing accounts and working collaboratively. Sales numbers associated with those accounts were deducted from my sales total without notification, yet my targets, which were based on previous sales from the same accounts, remained the same. Strike two!

Then came the real rub. I found out on my own that with the detracted sales numbers I only missed the bottom tier of my largest target by 0.042 percent (landmine six). Appointment requests were delayed and dodged, until finally I had a sit down with a Founder. I was trying to put myself in his shoes. Though we received our last round of funding around the time I was hired, and I knew we had plenty of funds in reserve given our burn rate, I asked to confirm we weren't struggling financially for good measure. He confirmed we were on solid financial footing. I explained that my team teed up those accounts that were detracted, reminded him that the sales targets were not adjusted to reflect the changed numbers (only the sales results were), and stated that the accounts deducted were our best accounts nationwide. It took some prodding, but a hint of truth finally came out. He expected overall sales to be moving at a more aggressive clip. I scratched my head. We were in triple digit growth. I'd transformed the sales organization, meeting sales targets that were mutually agreed upon. Then he mandated a pivot that I advised against and that sent growth in the opposite direction. It felt like he had buyer's remorse and insatiable expectations.

If I was in his shoes, he asked me, and there was a salesperson in front of him with the same scenario, what I would do? I told him sincerely and passionately that I would pay the agreed-upon bonus that was achieved because it would foster better collaboration during the strategic change. Given his comfort level, I told him, I personally would accept the modified numbers that put me at the lowest tier with much less financial reward. After we had that conversation and numerous follow ups, I was finally paid a portion of my bonus. That episode should have been strike three!

What can I say? I felt an obligation to support my sales team, and leaving during a volatile time would have been irresponsible and selfish. There were external signs pushing for my departure, too. I was being courted by recruiters. I waved them off, but there was a standout position I should have pursued, a position in my wheelhouse for a company in health tech I admired. Still, I passed on the opportunity and stuck it out where I was. My morale was the lowest it had ever been as a salesperson, including during those early years of feast or famine as a full commission rep. I dreaded going to work, and though I still was usually at the office a couple of hours before most everyone else, for the first time I found myself itching to leave by 5:30 p.m. to catch the ferry and gladly make the 90-minute commute home. My relationship with that Founder deteriorated. He openly discredited me in front of my team. The possibility of long-term employment at that company was doomed. Never underestimate the significance of the impact incentive pay can make.

CHAPTER 12

Sales Enablement

Sales enablement. What the hell is that?

Well, it's a relatively new way of describing all-encompassing sales force improvements. The goal of true sales enablement is to support salespeople to reach their pinnacle levels of performance. That way there are only superstars and when one leaves, a formula is applied to fill that slot with the next superstar. It means arming salespeople with the resources required to be successful. It means continuous and at times painstaking optimization to keep the tide rising to lift all ships.

In the recent past, sales force design was largely used to describe what is called sales enablement today. However, sales force design nowadays pertains to organizational structure, parsing out territories, and creating roadmaps that forecast sales force capacity and that are woven into the company's strategic intent. Sales enablement means all these things and also pertains to some of the things we already discussed, such as compensation incentive plans, measuring success with KPIs/leaderboards/dashboards, hiring based on sales context, and sales hire onboarding. Sales context is central to sales enablement; it's all about having a buyer-centric mindset and optimizing around that mindset.

Sales leaders use a vernacular that's worth understanding when referring to sales enablement. They talk about the ecosystem. For sales enablement the ecosystem pertains to all things that impact employee customer-facing engagement. Sales enablement aims to break down department silos and promote cross-functional collaboration. There are productivity tools (to be discussed in the tech stack chapter). Visibility, sales methodologies, training, and coaching all come into play. Constant reference to alignment, mainly to marketing, and references to customer success are to be expected when sales leaders are discussing the subject of sales enablement as well.

When sales leaders mention visibility in the sales-enablement context, they're referring to tracking activities of sales reps and buyers to gain insight. Content analytics identify levels of engagement for different types of marketing material, providing visibility on where to focus to create better-quality content. Opportunity pipeline tracking affords sales leaders the ability to visualize sales flow and address bottlenecks that may arise. Activity reports assist sales leaders in identifying productivity to improve process and procedure. Visibility therefore leads to improved productivity, planning, and execution.

Sales methodology is the way salespeople sell, and it's integral to the selling process, informing reps on the steps to follow in order to close the sale. Methodologies add structure to the sales process and can be adapted to the organization's unique sales process. However, they must fit the type of sale, and reps should use the methodology correctly. With so many sales methodologies available (we'll take a deep dive into them in a later chapter), sales leaders must distinguish the best fit for their sales organization.

Training and coaching are two different animals. Sales training should be thought of as a group activity, where an instructor has the class follow a series of updated modals. Coaching takes the form of one-on-one engagement, with the sales leader working with the rep, or the sales leader working with a small group to have reps work on specific inefficiencies. Reinforcement through repetition is key here. The most successful sales leaders I've worked with have introduced a change through a group training session, followed by no more than three areas to coach on each week for proficiency, leading to the most effective retention.

When the marketing team and the sales team have different goals, misalignment occurs. Marketing teams devote considerable resources to supporting sales teams with customer leads, content, and market insights. When both departments work as one team with revenue as the goal, magical things happen. High level collateral isn't enough, though, marketing needs to create supporting content for the entire buying process in order to reinforce what the salespeople are conveying to prospective buyers. Agreed upon parameters should permit salespeople to be prescriptive and sell to buyers' unique gaps. Marketing should closely monitor and review content analytics and optimize to help give sales a leg up. To be effective, sales must keep marketing in the loop about collateral used and inform marketing teams of frontline market intelligence. Sales should follow lead nurturing protocol with the support of marketing to increase the response rate of hibernating prospects. In the end, alignment with marketing is crucial to accelerated sales success and an undercurrent of sales enablement.

Customer success is about customer relationship retention and optimization. It means having an in-depth knowledge of the customer type, product or service expertise, and solid understanding of the market segment. The emerging customer success team is initially tasked with fighting churn and using data-driven decisions to proactively increase customer retention. While sales leaders in the context of sales enablement may refer to customer success as the value the company provides to satisfy and keep a customer loyal, distinct customer success teams that are hyper-focused on increasing retention are becoming commonplace in today's sales organizations.

Sales Process

When thinking about sales enablement, process is a core facet, particularly for inside sales organizations. Technology startups that provide valuable services will continuously update their product. That means the customer-facing platform and the backend tools reps use daily are constantly evolving. Patches may launch as frequently as twice a week, in fact. For this reason, process is often viewed as a waste of time. I disagree.

Fundamental process should remain in place. Following a process methodically provides sales leaders a basis for comparison in order to optimize and elevate the entire team through effectiveness assessments. Details will change until there is a major pivot, with hope informed and aligned with activity report data. Process fundamentals provide reps with an activity protocol that saves them time and allows them to navigate innately while handling customer interaction in real time. The multitasking nature of call centers warrants sales leaders to implement standard processes to reduce the chaos of the dynamic nature of customer interaction, while providing predictable steps that can be measured for improvement. As backend tools evolve, steps in the process can be modified to match. Sales leaders and upper management will want to know key metrics based on clean data that consistent process provides. KPIs such as win rate, time to revenue, transition rates, and bookings/closed deals, for instance, provide a sales score card for the organization that relies on good data. Without a process in place, reps are left to their own devices to succeed or fail, and visibility diminishes, in effect abandoning the primary tenet of sales enablement.

Field sales must have sales processes firmly in place. Medium and large companies will have more employees, and with the increase in headcount comes an increase in variable ways to conduct selling. Predictable, repeatable processes get all reps following the same tried and true format to get to closing the sale as quickly as possible. A predictable process flattens the learning curve for new hires and for employees who are promoted to new teams. Consequently, sales process is an imperative for medium and large companies to thrive.

Field sales reps have the luxury of autonomy, though sales process should be nonnegotiable. Going back to the arguments for visibility, sales leaders should draw a hard line on process. Reps can still be creative about tailoring their messages and getting to the buyer, much more so than inside sales that may be following playbook scripts closely. The process tied into the sales methodology needs to be followed closely to identify what's working and what's not across the field sales organization. The biggest resistance sales leaders will get from reps (other than comp-related discussions) is anything that perceivably hamstrings their creative sales efforts. Additionally, field reps need to know there is *no wiggle room* when it comes to process. To garner support, sales leaders must acknowledge reps who are crushing it and give those reps the floor to discuss how aspects of the process are working well for them. This gives those in the trenches more credence and confidence.

Sales leaders who hold new hires accountable from day one, forcing them to follow process, will find these reps rarely deviate from sales process in the future. Unless it's a new sales force being built from zero, getting new reps trained well to follow process and proving results, can be advantageous for sales leaders to support their case in following process for the rest of the team. In the end, outside sales should expect that following sales process is company mandated, as following process helps them and their coworkers get better at selling. The mantra: trust the process!

The Value of Methodical Process

Once I was tasked with converting a call center of customer service reps who followed inconsistent process into process-driven inside sales reps. The challenge before me was the stigma associated with sales as opposed to customer service, the relative autonomy the reps had to handle customer conversations, and the challenge of getting overall process buy-in. Working to my advantage was the fact the reps were dedicated employees in an ever-changing startup environment with a strong work ethic. They were also backed by a smart general manager (GM) who was on the same page as me and saw the value of process improvements.

Working closely with the GM, we implemented process improvements by dividing and conquering. The GM had a solid background on the tech stack and was a key stakeholder in backend tool improvements. So, she was put in charge of optimizing the use of the backend tools for the sales staff. Capturing customer information, navigating profiles on the other side of the marketplace, and searching subject matter in the course of a single customer interaction caused reps to toggle between numerous windows without defined processes. Once the GM identified processes that shaved costly minutes off using the backend tools and reduced toggling distractions, she had a small team pilot the changes. After statistically significant and relevant data proving the efficacy of the changes started coming in, the staff was trained and coached on the process improvements.

Simultaneously, I worked on the sales process. This involved everything from having one-on-one conversations about the importance of selling in order to break down the wall created by the traditional salesperson stigma, to coaching reps using basic sales techniques for better conversations through each step in the process. Within the broader sales process were microprocesses that reps had to be convinced to follow. Process baby steps were homed in on with the hope that larger processes would be adhered to and produce a well-oiled machine.

Response rate was a key metric given our volume and how much we seemingly were leaving on the table. To zero in on one aspect of response rate, I had a small group of talented reps experiment with leaving voicemails that followed a completely different process. Cadence and tempo aside, the major change we tested was leading with relevance.

Rather than beginning the message with the reps introducing their name, followed by the company name and their contact number, we had reps lead with relevance, succinctly referring to the interest the customer had initially conveyed. At the very end of the call the reps mentioned their phone number, name, and finally the company. We saw a large uptick with this approach. So much so that we had statistically relevant proof to get buy-in with the rest of the reps, ultimately improving response rates on voicemails by approximately 35 percent.

The same process was followed with initial customer calls where a live customer answered the phone. It may seem simple, but getting reps to do something different than what they'd been raised since they were children to do and then follow a seemingly counter-intuitive process was a *huge* challenge. Before long, reps started accepting the idea of leading with relevance rather than introducing themselves before jumping into the purpose of the call. Doing so became innate after repetition, leading to better sales outcomes.

To further increase response rate, we ran a regression analysis to gain insight on the best process to follow. Using observational data with a population of >20,000 logged prospective customers, we excluded seasonality and collected the data randomly to prevent potential bias. Our summary statistics were based on variable categorical types that were being used within the parameters of the seven contact points required before marking a lead dormant. We had enough data and anecdotal evidence to know seven attempts for responses was threshold before we reached the point of diminishing returns. What we didn't know was the overall process to accelerate the response rate. The results were presented in the form of charts where the summary statistics clearly illustrated that the top three processes that yielded the best results were responding to customer inquiries within an hour of initial contact, best time of day and days to follow up with prospects, and mode of follow up. Variable pay was tied into metrics like response time, getting reps to respond within 30 minutes >75 percent of the time for example. The core drivers to achieve the greatest ROI for sales efforts were objectively proven, process was designed around them, and the team was bought in to implementing them partly due to the proof, and partly due to the compensation tie in.

Process change is also behavioral change. When a significant change in process creates a large performance lever that warrants sales rep adaptation, behavior modification is required.

How do you break old habits and get reps to adopt new habits? Leverage the competitive spirits of reps with a contest until the new behavior becomes ingrained. Used selectively, sales contests will change behavior. Contests are generally used more broadly to go after dormant leads, new customer acquisition, or customer groups—but they can also be used sparingly for process improvements that really move the needle. The contest leaderboard stats produce ample motivation for reps to change the process and strive to win the contest to reap the financial rewards and bragging rights. After the contest is over, the process becomes ingrained, and the reps can set their sights on other improvements.

It was gratifying to see the transformation of that office. When it began, reps were doing things differently, saying things inconsistently, and producing unpredictable results. Through methodical process adherence, customer service individuals were turned into high functioning inside sales reps who worked uniformly and produced predictable results. Process brought order to chaos and reduced anxiety, affording reps to be their best at their jobs. The team in tune and singing off the same hymn sheet was a wonderful sight to behold.

The Sales Playbook

Along the lines of process is advocation for the sales playbook. I've heard sales professionals say that the sales playbook is gospel. I'm not convinced that any playbook is the holy grail for sales. The business is constantly changing, and so is the playbook. The playbook is nothing more than a reference piece. Execution determines the result.

Good training and coaching through repetition are much more effective than a static playbook in a dynamic environment. More than anything, the playbook functions as a springboard through the different sales stages and customer conversations that reps can use as a quick reference should an anomaly in the usual process occur.

The process itself should be second nature after thousands of repetitions. The playbook itself is nice to have, particularly for employees in new roles still in onboard mode.

Enabling Sales Leaders

For orientation, the head of sales spends time with reps, but to drive business results the head of sales works closely with sales leaders. Sales leaders get caught up putting out fires regardless of how proactive an organization may try to be. Doing so gets them off task, and over time sales leaders may end up focusing on the wrong things. The head of sales or the layer above the front-line sales leader must frequently assess sales leaders on core competencies, leadership, coaching, hiring, and accountability.

Measuring sales leadership effectiveness is a part of sales enablement that must not go ignored. Bellwethers include the amount of mistakes reps are making and how quickly those mistakes are corrected, team morale, and rep engagement. Anonymous surveys that solicit the input of direct reports on their leaders serve as a great gauge on leadership effectiveness.

A world class Silicon Valley life sciences enterprise tied variable pay into the results of their leadership audits to keep sales leaders focused on worthy topics that had measurable behavior and impact. Each year there were biannual surveys that had themes for the year reinforcing strategic intent. Leaders' results from direct reports were evaluated in part based on external global benchmarks, and a dashboard was provided publicly within the company to provide result transparency. While leaders who made grade in these audits benefited financially, those with consistently high scores were recognized as highly effective leaders and put on track for career advancement. Leaders with consistently low scores were paired with and mentored by high – scoring, effective leaders. It wasn't all about the scores, though. The results identified areas for improvement and put leadership top of mind for those with direct report responsibility.

A company doesn't need to have tens of thousands of employees across continents to warrant leadership audits. Smaller scale versions can be implemented to gauge leadership effectiveness and spot opportunities for leadership development. The takeaway here is that sales leaders at every level must be measured on their leadership effectiveness and provided the opportunity to improve their leadership skills for the better of the organization and its employees.

Coaching is an impactful part of leadership, particularly when done correctly. Good sales coaches are recognized for their ability to use the sales process and tech stack for meaningful coaching sessions that lead to improvements. They can identify skill gaps with individual team members and create development plans to fill those gaps. They have little employee turnover and are effective at onboarding new team members. Instead of taking over one-off situations, good coaches look for teachable moments to encourage open skills for reps to make connections through knowledge, empowering reps to match a strategy to a problem autonomously. They coach reps on how best to close the sale without taking over the sale themselves and acting as super sales-people. Good coaching is reflective of the caliber of sales reps on the team and is hard to miss.

Sales leaders must be measured on hiring as well. How closely do they follow the hiring process and interview methodology? Can they inspire candidates? Can they shorten the learning curve to get new sales reps up to speed efficiently and effectively? The amount of time and resources committed to sales hiring justifies the attention senior leadership must dedicate to monitoring the core competency is in line with standards.

The final core competency that requires ongoing monitoring is holding sales leaders accountable to what they are tracking, role model behavior, and to keeping everyone in adherence to process and procedure. Team members with a sales leader strong on accountability will be able to articulate successful outcomes and failures. Team members will be able to convey mutual accountability, and how well their sales leader sticks to commitments. The sales leader will have leading and lagging indicators at the front of their minds at any given time that can be conveyed at the drop of a hat. The sales leader will be able to artic-ulate the reasons KPIs are being tracked and where the team stands. Measuring accountability also diagnoses work capacity: is the sales team barely coming up for air; do they need additional support; are they being underutilized?

Just as sales leaders provide ongoing coaching and development for direct reports, so should the head of sales. The head of sales monitors core competencies and also develops sales leaders into superstars. Additionally, the head of sales can review specific coaching initiatives; provide insights on KPIs; and get sales leaders involved in marketing campaigns, changes to rep incentive plans, and motivate sales leaders to sell the company vision. Since sales leaders are creating sales multipliers, it stands to reason that the head of sales would invest time and resources into getting sales leaders to reach their full potential.

Scale

Companies that expand too fast without cracking the code on sales enablement tend to implode.

Investors, and in turn Founders, want to see results immediately in startup environments. In growth environments, the Board and the company with new executive leadership may need to drive shareholder earnings to make a statement that the management changes are setting the company on the right course.

The pressure for results often pushes companies to expand prematurely, and the small cracks in the dam become large fissures as the organization grows and the problems grow with it. It takes a super salesperson to convince company Founders, Investors, and new Executives to stand down until kinks are worked out prior to expansion.

There are emotional and financial risks as well resulting from premature expansion. What do you think happens to all those employees who were hired only to be let go a year later? What does that do to your core talent pool, and what message does that send to the market? The investment in training new staff members, purchasing tools to expand the tech stack to support the larger sales org, and increases in office overhead can sink a company. Things end badly when companies scale too soon. Conversely, when company decision makers have patience and are objective about the decision to scale, expectations are exceeded.

Through the iterative process of sales enablement, group refinements will be made, and a formula will emerge using a core group of sales reps. Selling through the sales stages and optimizing to sales contexts, before long processes become codified. A measured approach to hiring tests the ramp up process and new hires surpass performance or meet the bar of existing hires in short order. Across the sales organization there are repeatable and predictable results on a consistent basis. Then is the time to scale!

CHAPTER 13

Tech Stack

In sales enablement, technology is the sales leader's friend, just as long as sales leaders are selective about the technology implemented. Salespeople (especially those in the field) generally struggle to embrace technological improvements. They get comfortable with what they already use and are resistant to change.

I mention this because often sales leaders believe that inclusion of new tool rollouts in the business plan will lead to generating greater sales growth. What is forgotten is that the best sales support tools in the world won't work unless they fit the sales team, address a true problem for improvement, and are able to be adopted by sales staff. Once again, the sales leader will need to gain buy-in, the sales leader must sell the solution and be careful what technology to invest in.

Here are two commonly used phrases coming from sales professionals that test my patience: *the product sells itself* and *if only we had . . .* When reps make the comment, *the product (or service) sells itself,* I get the urge to say, "then why do we need to pay you?" The other is stated, usually as a result of tracking below or missing goals. *If only we had* another new widget with these bells and whistles, I could crush my numbers.

Reps who bring those phrases and that mindset over as sales leaders make excuses for bad team execution. *If only we had* a simpler CRM. *If only we had* software to better equip our salespeople.

To curtail effort required to gain true buy-in, sales leaders tell salespeople, *the product sells itself.* Sales professionals who work with what they have and make a conscious effort to sell without falling back on those phrases find themselves leading their respective fields.

The main point is salespeople want to augment their sales efforts with tools for support. They will blame lack of something missing from the sales enablement arsenal and their product offering. It is up to sales leaders to distinguish petty demands based on excuses from essential technology that is rooted on objective assessments with solutions that will leverage the sales force against threats or assist them with opportunities.

Questions sales leaders should ask are:

- What problem needs solving?
- What are the costs of leaving that problem unresolved?
- Do we have the capacity to integrate the solution?

A mid-sized company that was expanding its sales team casted a wide net to source as many candidates as possible. Without enough bandwidth to handle the incoming resumes, limited resources were dedicating most of their time filtering qualified from unqualified applicants for the open roles and doing little else of value for the organization.

I suggested a simple and inexpensive software solution: an applicant tracking system (ATS). The ATS scanned applicant resumes automatically using key terms that were essential to the ideal candidate profile based on the sales context. Immediately upon implementation, limited resources had bandwidth to focus on other high value tasks, including setting up phone screens for the few applicants that passed muster based on key terms.

In this case:

- The problem was an abundance of unqualified candidates were applying for the role and we didn't have the human resources to stay ahead of qualifying candidates.
- The costs were considerable, estimated at 70 percent of salary for two employees at $3,000 a week, instead of bringing in revenue at a net positive of > $1,000 a week (total cost per week was therefore > $4,000).
- Software integration was quick and intuitive, hardware was already functioning and available for use.

"It's A No Brainer!"

You may be tempted to say that as a sales professional. Perhaps when hearing that expression, it seems innocent enough. The fact is saying something is a no brainer is equivalent to telling someone, "duh!"

I have firsthand experience that using that phrase can have detrimental consequences. Thanks to that experience, I never said it again in a professional setting, especially when attempting to add to our company's tech stack.

It was early on in my sales career, I was calling on a distributor that, together with his partner, were formerly end users supplying users from the same target group they were once part of with products. I had a good relationship with Luke, one of the partners closer to me in age and with similar interests. We had a promotion for products that were in their wheelhouse and a great fit for their customers, payment terms were precisely what they asked for, the discount for the buy-in was reasonable, it was a guaranteed order I thought. At the end of my presentation I said to Luke, "It's a no brainer!" His face turned red, he stood up, and after calling me several names that will go unmentioned, he asked me to leave, he said he could never work with me again. It was in the late 90s when that happened, and I still remember the look on his red face even today! Aside from losing what I thought was an easy purchase order, I had to deal with his partner going forward and when they were together in the same room, Luke wouldn't even acknowledge my presence, making it uncomfortable for me each time. What was once a thriving, top-20 account, died on the vine.

The moral of the story: unless you want to run the risk of ruining relationships by implying someone is stupid by referring to something as a "no brainer," sales professionals should refrain from using that phrase with customers, channel partners, and coworkers. This is particularly relevant when it comes to selling a technology solution to upper management, or to reps to garner support. Instead stick to the utility of the solution, how it will bring in more revenue or reduce costs, and how easily it can be integrated. Let your audience determine if it truly is a no brainer based on the facts you have presented and your influence in conveying those facts.

A Note on Adoption

Adoption is the top reason sales tools succeed or fail[xxvi]. The legacy of a predecessor's investment can be a heavy burden for the organization. Money keeps being thrown at the problem and reps hate having it forced down their throats. The team must be committed to using the solution. They must be bought in. They must also be properly trained and have the capacity to learn. There must be a meticulous rollout plan including reinforcement events to drive adoption home.

Taking it a step further, good sales leaders monitor usage with metrics. Usage monitoring will shed light on what part of the solution is not being adopted, and who needs the most coaching to get up to speed.

The data also helps sales leaders when selling up and helps inform future tech-adoption planning. Sales enablement tracks everything else—why not track new tool adoption?

Systems, Systems, Systems

How do you tell the difference between a new business with a young staff versus a mature business with an aging demographic?

Systems.

Coming from a mature company with long-time use of few systems, the biggest challenge some sales leaders find themselves experiencing is technological adoption to various cutting-edge systems. This is where the selective piece matters, as having systems in place that really bring value to the organization can be a boon.

In many fledgling companies, the proliferation of technology leads to a proliferation of systems that are disjointed and have the inverse effect of making work more efficient. Many solutions offer free trials or free packages with bare essentials that are adopted as part of an organization's support arsenal without providing that much incremental value yet hindering workflow and taxing employee bandwidth requiring usage.

For employees coming from mature companies, the adoption expectation for the multitude of systems is borderline unrealistic. Speaking from personal experience, I found myself being the old guy (in my early 40s) who had difficulty learning the systems used at our tech company. In fact, it was my biggest challenge for the first six months I was aboard. Then again, I had some coworkers there refer to songs from the 80s as "The Classics," they were in diapers when I was cresting my first million-dollar quota.

Fledgling or mature, having cutting edge technological solutions just for the sake of having them doesn't make much business sense. It is easy for sales enablement to get caught up in trends rather than make objective assessments based on needs. The litmus test is if the technological solution will bring quantifiable results, if there is true utility with the solution, otherwise sales enablement should pass. Being mindful of striking a balance with only essential technology implementation, there are some great options for system consideration these days that help to optimize the work environment.

Using a wide lens, the organization tends to adopt technology across functions and make it fit for the sales organization as well. In startup environments, the solutions that are free or have a low cost to entry are embraced first. For collaboration, Slack is the go-to. For project management, Trello may be favored with Mac users, and Microsoft Project for PC users. For business intelligence platforms, Tableau or Sisense may be used. For file sharing, Drop Box or Google Docs. G Suite for productivity and collaboration. If using G Suite, Copper CRM is probably the logical choice. Payroll and benefits, likely Gusto or Paychex. Hootsuite for social media marketing. For recruitment, Lever. Not to mention a host of sales specific tools, some of which we'll run through now.

VoIP

Voice Over IP (VoIP), also known as IP telephony, has replaced traditional phone systems in call centers. Instead of using public-switched telephone networks, computers dial out and receive calls via the internet. Voice and data networks can be run over a single network. That combined with other cost savings features like lower cost extensions makes VoIP significantly less expensive than traditional copper wire telephone systems. Between accessibility, cost, and flexibility, VoIP has eclipsed traditional phone systems. The disadvantages are internet bandwidth or strong connections must be maintained, and the same security vulnerability as anything that is exposed through the internet pertains to VoIP. The tradeoffs make business sense, though.

This leads us to contact center operations software. In addition to voice calls, these solutions provide reporting and analytics, engagement and productivity tools, and multichannel communications. The technology assists sales leaders in call monitoring and provides reps with tools for customer management that are integrated into the backend tools. There are considerations when selecting the right call center as a service (CCaaS) solution for the organization, local presence being one of them.

Local presence is a system that allows reps to automatically call customers using local area codes. In terms of response rate, there is a considerable uptick in connection rates when using a familiar area code, prospects are more likely to pick up the phone, hence the importance of CCaaS solutions with local presence. In most cases, batched phone numbers from various area codes are selected and charged for use in order to satisfy the local presence requirement. My only experience with a dynamic local presence CCaaS was with Talkdesk. Outbound caller ID would feature hyperlocal phone numbers optimized automatically to increase connection rates. If the business demands phone call prospecting, CCaaS with solid local presence is essential. Though other multichannel communications may make local presence less important, or there may be other considerations when choosing the right CCaaS for the business.

There are a host of features to consider including latency, provisioning, data tracking, and capacity limitations. Call latency, where the voice on the other end lags and jitter occurs, can be conversation killers. Solutions with direct media delivery improves call quality and reduces latency. New seats will be required as new hires are made, or team structure changes. Seamlessly adding lines without impacting capacity is a must. For monitoring marketing campaigns, dedicated toll-free phone numbers may be required for tracking purposes, so a simplified porting and provisioning process is a serious consideration. Business insights are critical for sales enablement. Tracking call data is essential as it ties closely into activity goals and helps sales leaders optimize around patterns. Last major consideration, selecting a solution that has unlimited capacity as you scale without being charged for unused capacity. Communication systems with limits will lead to blocked calls during peak times at full capacity, so in addition to expansion considerations, the solution must have unlimited call channels.

Real time analytics, flexibility, intuitive integration, and cost are other factors sales-enablement leaders should consider. Aircall, which ticks all these boxes, is a worthy contender. Additionally, Aircall has a solid reputation for being consistent with less dropped calls, a common drawback of VoIP. Integration with backend tools or CRM may limit choices as well. Going with a robust CCaaS will narrow the field for the right choice for the unique business requirements. If sales leaders desire to integrate systems, going with a feature rich CCaaS like RingCentral may be the best fit. There are scores of CCaaS, just about all of which offer free trials. Before committing, having a couple of tech savvy reps open to change test them out along with sales leaders, is a prudent auditing process that will increase the likelihood of picking the right solution for the business.

Managing Remote Reps

More companies are moving away from location-based office spaces in lieu of virtual call centers where reps can be located anywhere. Up until a few years ago, having supervisors oversee call center employees in order to coach, train, and keep everyone honest was a business necessity. With the advent of various sales enablement tools, the option to hire remote sales reps spread across geography and that report into a virtual call center is growing in popularity. The advantages of remote call center reps include a bigger hiring pool of candidates to source from, natural time zone alignment, and lower overhead cost without leasing of office space plus the costs that come with it. In-house call centers are challenging enough to keep reps performing at a high level, technology has to be that good to be just as effective for remote reps to perform at a high caliber.

There is no reason why CCaaS cannot be used remotely. In fact, much of the technology mentioned in this chapter can be applied to remote reps. They will be logging in to the company VPN anyway, just physically from different locations. Activity reports, call analytics, sales tracking, all of it can be done virtually. The challenge until the last couple of years was effective coaching. Technology has solved that as well. For example, Cogito improves the quality of rep interaction by providing live behavioral guidance. Technology that improves soft skills is welcome at any call center, but also opens up the option for rep development remote and real time. Until recently I was a skeptic, particularly when it came to the bonding effects of face-to-face human interaction and developing a high-performance culture. Those issues can be addressed in creative ways through biannual sales meetings and team-building activities. Thanks to the support provided by technology, virtual call centers made up of remote reps merits consideration.

Robo Dialers—The Good, The Bad, And the Ugly

In the United States, robo calls have become ubiquitous. Companies use these to automatically dial phone numbers in mass, connect the answered call to a message or transfer to a live agent. For the record, I'm not a fan. The phone rings interrupting a thought, conversation, or a drive. A few seconds in it becomes frustratingly obvious it is a robo call—no, I'm not interested in your time share opportunity! Unfortunately, robo dialers have been abused and it has come to a point where legislation is being considered to prohibit use, probably in part because politicians are also robo call victims.

Although not a personal favorite, robo calls do have legitimate business function when used correctly and should not be completely ruled out. For example, if a side of the marketplace has members that have opted-in to receiving agent calls for opportunities (e.g. matching professionals providing a service with end users), robo dialers make business sense. In that scenario, the sales team may get a short list of twenty qualified professionals in proximity to the end customers, the robo dialer simultaneously, or in batches, dials out to all of them and transfers the answered calls to live agents. Another viable use is for announcements. If that expensive machine you just bought, or that bag of veggies purchased from the wholesale store has an urgent recall, robo dialers can efficiently notify the customer population before something disastrous occurs.

Like so many other things in sales, use of robo dialers must fit the sales context. Where companies go astray is when they look at absolute conversion numbers and use robo dialers as lead gen vehicles. Working at a company with a two-sided marketplace, I was forced to voice the robo dialer topic with a couple of trusted sales leaders after giving in to the incessant requests from one of the Founders. Without expressing my views to prevent bias, I stated how the robo dialers may benefit the business by keeping reps on the phone with a steady stream of incoming calls and what that may translate to in additional revenue. Funny, both sales leaders looked at me in disbelief and said, "Really, are you serious?" They weren't even willing to run an experiment! Good for them, they drew a hard line and along my concerns, given our sales context we would have lost customers in the long run through the experience in lieu of short-term gain. There are situations where using robo dialers is a viable option. However, in most circumstances, robo dialers are not used appropriately and the badgering that results leads to bad customer experiences associated with the company brand and translates into lost customers or lower customer lifetime value.

Customer Relationship Management (CRM)

CRM can be used for good or evil—at least that's the rep perspective. Arguably the hardest thing to garner uniform support for, CRM is an integral tool for the sales organization. When used correctly it helps sales professionals stay on top of client relationships, managing pipeline stages, and keeping organized in a fluid environment. For organizations, CRM stands for continuity resource material, providing redundancy so critical information that the company invested in is available and not lost. Having said this, especially remote and field sales reps, see CRM as big brother that infringes on their autonomy. To a certain extent, they are right, though the motivation is to improve efficiency and effectiveness, rather than to spy on employees.

In the early 2000s, CRM had evolved and gained traction from the previous decade. Nowadays, there are numerous options that range from free CRM with basic service offerings, to elaborate highly customized systems for enterprise clients. The big three from the early 2000s are still leading the field, including Oracle, MS Dynamics, and Salesforce. There has been speculation from many a techie founder that CRM leaders like Salesforce are on a rapid decline. With dominant market share, CCaaS integrations essentially designed for them, and the $1 billon Salesforce Tower that breaks through the clouds of the San Francisco skyline at over 1,000 feet in elevation, indications are otherwise. Offshoots, copycats, and niche CRM offerings now exist to accommodate business needs no matter how different the business may be or how limited the budget.

CRM works by pulling in information from various sources (email, voice, social media) into a single place to organize workflows and business processes. Tracking all that data allows for task automation, machine learning and analytics to do the heavy lifting for sales professionals. Assigned teams have access to the information so they can collaborate more effectively, provide better customer experiences, and produce faster outcomes.

Here's a scenario based on a real-life example of CRM: a new customer bought an expensive product that is not working correctly, so they connect with inside sales to verify the product was the right one for the application. The rep notes the customer's details, including the application and the customer's complaints about the product. With the product verified as correct for the application, she transfers the customer to the service department where the service technician reviews the notes from the rep and picks up where she left off. He performs a diagnostic over the phone and determines that a faulty electronic component is the culprit. He accesses the local sales rep's calendar while the customer is still on the phone and blocks off time for a visit with the customer on a day when the rep will already be in the area. The tech also leaves notes for the rep that provide suggestions on cross selling of accessories and consumables the customer has not purchased and will need for the application. Just as with this event, CRM allows employees to work in concert to deliver exceptional customer service and increase company revenue.

CRM falls into three main categories: analytical, collaborative, and operational. As the name implies, the main function of analytical CRM is data analysis. Insights help upper management make better strategic decisions, inform sales leaders on sales effectiveness, and sheds light on the impact of marketing campaigns. Collaborative CRM is designed to enable business units across an organization to access customer information to improve customer service across functions, encourage customer loyalty, and increase sales through new customer acquisition. Operational CRM automates the sales process to generate sales leads and capture all the required details for service during the customer lifecycle. The current and future strategy of the business as well as the size of the organization factor into the type of CRM and the system to be implemented.

CRM Implementation

Businesses with three or more salespeople must have CRM. Speed to opportunity is key and competitors in the same space are likely going to be faster because they have supporting technology, they have CRM. Businesses are more likely to have a CRM system and the transition to a new system or addons are more widely accepted from sales staff than in the past when CRM was uncommon and viewed more as novelty. New businesses integrating into a first time CRM system face adoption obstacles, there are ways to make the road to adoption less treacherous.

We had narrowed down the CRM systems we were going to go with to Salesforce and MS Dynamics. After a brief trial, most of us leaned toward Salesforce. But because the international consensus from other subsidiaries was for MS Dynamics, we committed to join the multinational subsidiaries and adopt the same CRM. It was a logical choice, we would learn from each other about effective adoption and experiment with customization, collaborating on the ultimate system for the business across borders. Well, it took several years just for all the reps across continents to adopt the system.

We learned from our European colleagues that had limited user adoption and as a result, had put in place ultimatums for use. In North America, we wanted to avoid impacting the company culture with such a heavy-handed approach, so we selectively trained a core group of reps with the goal of having them advocate for the CRM adoption.

While this group included a couple of tech savvy reps that had previous CRM experience, it also included the least tech savvy rep of the entire organization and our most outspoken rep. We partnered the tech savvy reps with the reps that needed the most technical help until everyone reached a level of proficiency that was acceptable to be used as resources for other reps. We adopted short instructional videos from our overseas colleagues and created text as well as audio instructions to support various learning styles across our sales organization.

At our national sales meeting, I introduced the CRM system, provided the benefits of the technology for the sales force, outlined the reason why world class sales organizations are already using CRM, listed which of our competitors were ahead of the field with the help of CRM, and called out specific upcoming functionality that would directly benefit reps on a daily basis (such as route planning). I mentioned the pilot team had been using it for the last few months and opened the floor for them to provide the broader group with their feedback based on their experiences. The least tech savvy rep of the pilot group started first, describing how quickly he learned how to navigate the system and the benefits he saw. Then the outspoken rep chimed in. We had to cut him off after thirty minutes. We broke up the teams into small groups and introduced them to the content available with a timetable for adoption plus mentorship pairings as they went about learning the system based on their individual schedules. It is safe to say that our sales team adopted the CRM system faster and with less resistance then the other subsidiaries around the world.

Compensation Management Software

Compensation Management Software systems are a boon. For most of my sales leadership career we reinvented the wheel using excel workbooks that had occasional circular errors and certainly didn't have the advantages of robust compensation management systems.

Those advantages include easily modifying compensation plans, forecasting employee variable pay, and quickly making pay adjustments. Compensation data reporting and administrative dashboards are additional benefits. For small businesses, compensation management software can be used as a stand-alone system or integrated for medium to large organizations as part of the HR suite of products.

With incentive compensation a significant driver of desired behavior, using professional compensation management software designed specifically around variable pay is a worthy business investment. Systems such as Xactly reduce comp design downtime and provide sales leaders with the confidence to roll-out compensation incentive plans supported by a professional third-party software system. They provide the ability to benchmark plans across industry, iterate on more effective plan design, and identify potential performance issues. The benefit of these systems to pay accurately offsets costs required to subscribe to the software.

Learning Management Systems (LMS)

The resource heavy nature of salesperson training has created a need for learning management systems as a solution. An LMS is a software application that provides customized learning formats that can be tailored to specific roles. LMS helps solve issues associated with administrating, documenting, and structuring training programs.

LMS offers the advantage of systemized learning reinforcement using a microlearning approach to ensure the most important material in the training session sticks. Proficiency tracking, quizzes, and certifications are usually included in the bundle. The time saved with a streamlined training program and the effective reinforcement LMS produces are the reasons more companies are utilizing LMS.

Sales Asset Management (SAM)

SAM software is designed to align sales and marketing teams, optimize marketing effectiveness, and increase sales effectiveness. Organizations benefit from having a central repository of all content and a system to help manage, analyze, and deliver content. SAM mitigates mistakes of using the wrong or outdated marketing materials, reduces or eliminates rep time creating content, and prompts reps to use the right content at the right time.

Sales Coaching Tools

Sales coaching tools in the form of software is gaining wider acceptance. It provides reps with structured practice sessions based on coaching from their sales leaders, that grades individuals and provides feedback. These applications analyze conversations and identify coachable moments to align reps with sales methodology and say the right things to drive revenue. Sales coaching software applications help sales leaders to level up all reps to the same high standard, empower reps to take the initiative to improve through self-coaching, and allows reps to benchmark their performance against that of their peers that have the greatest impact on closing the sale. This technology is pertinent for companies that have established a predictable, and repeatable sales process that is effective, and with scale they will augment technological support to get the sales force in lockstep at an accelerated rate.

Sales Engagement Platforms (SEP)

When high volume and low value deals require a customized repeatable process, sales enablement leaders turn to Sales Engagement Plat forms. An emerging category for sales organizations, SEP auto logs to CRM reducing administrative tasks for reps, directs the use of impactful content with customers, and provides insights on next steps in the sales process. It automates part of the workflow to accurately sequence with content across multiple touchpoints. When used correctly, SEP creates faster more impactful sales cycles and provides data on account engagement for optimization.

Sales Productivity Tools

When redundant low value tasks are affecting productivity, organizations turn to sales-productivity tools. Repetitive activities such as sending emails and setting up meetings can be automated using sales-productivity tools. Some sales-productivity tools also provide triggers for reps when leads take high intent actions such as landing on the company website. Additionally, they provide email tracking, sequencing, and workflow automation. Sales productivity tools reduce the time spent on low value tasks so that reps can maximize the time they spend having sales conversations.

Sales Readiness Tools

Often confused with sales enablement, sales readiness is verifying that reps have the expertise and skills required to have effective sales conversations throughout the buyer's journey. Readiness tools support this goal by measuring training completion and certifying that reps are meeting company standard with their skills and knowledge. Sales readiness tools provide structured frameworks for rep onboarding, training, and coaching specific to the buyer's journey. When done right, sales readiness tools prepare reps to have the greatest chance of success in closing more and bigger value deals.

The Perfect Tech Stack

Spoiler alert, there is no one size fits all. If it were that simple, anyone could be the head of sales. Rather, careful consideration of the business needs, rep capabilities, and where the company is headed, weigh in on deciding what technology to incorporate into the tech stack. The good news is there are a plethora of technological solutions that accelerate sales performance and offer variety to most accurately fit the unique sales context of the business to create the perfect tech stack.

Much of what these technologies provide can be done manually and accomplished with sweat equity, I know, I've done it myself before these offerings existed. Doing so is cheap, highly prescriptive, but also inefficient and comes with significant limitations. In today's competitive selling environment, companies serious about growth and creating a sales force that is repeatable, predictable, and scalable are required to invest in a tech stack that is aligned with the company's requirements.

CHAPTER 14

Sales Methodology

S ales methodologies are comprised of guiding principles to help salespeople successfully navigate steps within the sales process. They answer the "how," "what," and "why" of the sales process.

Adopting a sales methodology is important to the organization not only in order to prepare salespeople for effective communication through the sales process, but to ensure reps are doing and saying similar things in the right way at the right time. Sales methodologies offer a systematic approach to the seemingly unpredictable nature of human behavior. Typically, the sales methodology is driven by the head of sales directly and through an external consultant with expertise. Sales methodologies square with the business objectives and underscore sales effectiveness.

Sales Methodology Versus Sales Training

There are sales methodologies that are considered to be complete selling systems in that they also offer sales training. For example, a part of the methodology may be to provide corporate insights in a specific stage in the sales process. In this case, the sales training can reinforce nuance on delivering the sales conversation. This isn't to say that seemingly complete methodologies are better than methodologies that are exclusive of sales training since reps bring their own skills with them or companies have selective sales training programs tailored to their sales contexts.

Something else of note is that sales training, arguable more than anything else, gives reps confidence and provides them with bench-marks to strive for to become polished sales professionals. Whereas the sales methodology provides markers on when to interject in the sales process.

Familiar Sales Methodologies

The Challenger Sale is a methodology that, at its core, is designed to disrupt the way customers think about solving a business problem. Not all reps have the attributes required to be challengers. In fact, based on statistically relevant survey results, The Challenger Sale categorizes salespeople into five distinct sales rep profiles and identifies charac-teristics of each, ranking which rep profile is better aligned to be successful. Spoiler alert: it's the Challenger profile where reps are willing to lead with business insights (teach) that are prescriptive (tailor) to the buyer, and strategically guide (take control) the customer along the buying process.

The Challenger Sale is considered to be incomplete by some, yet comprehensive by others. It's comprehensive in the sense that CEB, now Gartner, offers everything from salesperson assessments and development plans, to rollout strategies supported with rollout teams for hire. For successful implementation of The Challenger Sale, the methodology transcends departments, and marketing collateral must reflect the sales methodology in line with what salespeople in the organization are communicating to customers. Furthermore, understanding the customer in detail that goes beyond high-level personas is critical for The Challenger Sale methodology to be successful. Marketing is on the hook for providing insights that are poignant for the customer and the sales organization. There is a wealth of resources to help with implementation, and companies that are selling complex products or services find success using this methodology. What Challenger has not offered is sales training, so some consider it incomplete. For complex, consensus selling, The Challenger Sale is a popular and effective choice.

Inbound Selling is based on pulling customers into the buying process through marketing analytics. Sales interactions are personalized based on page view analysis, social media engagement, and other areas. Inbound selling is gaining popularity with the rise of buyers who are purchasing through the internet and actively involved with social media.

Inbound reps create opportunities for buyers to engage the company where the company in turn creates prescriptive messaging to influence customers forward to purchase. Buyers and reps tend to favor this approach since it eliminates the use of sales scripts that may come off as canned, and it empowers reps to treat each customer uniquely based on their needs.

Miller Heiman Group incorporates Conceptual Selling and Strategic Selling into their sales methodologies. Conceptual selling is predicated on salespeople selling concepts or solutions, rather than products or services. Through tactful questioning, active listening, and empathy, the seller can tailor the solution in the context of the buyer's needs. Strategic selling utilizes the iconic blue sheet and helps simplify the complex sale, while providing a framework on approaching different stages of the sales process. The combination of the two make for a complete sales methodology.

MEDDIC stands for Metrics, Economic buyer, Decision criteria, Decision process, Identify Pain, and Champion. This sales methodology is highly structured and data driven. The end goal is to find the champion at a client's organization to act as an advocate for the rep's products or services. It is best applied for complex and enterprise selling. Using highly qualifying leads in a structured manner to get to the right person to make the sale is core to this methodology.

NEAT selling was developed by The Harris Group and Sales Hacker. It is a qualification framework updated for today's buying environment. NEAT stands for Need, Economic Impact, Access to Authority, and Timeline.

The NEAT acronym means more than what is on the surface. The "N" in NEAT stands for "need" with keen focus on pain points that reps must uncover during the sales conversation. "E" (economic impact) reminds reps to illustrate the economic impact the customer will realize when they make a change versus their current state. "A" (access to authority) refers to the person who will champion the rep's product or service and have influence on the ultimate decision maker. "T" (for timeline) pertains to a compelling event or creating a sense of urgency so the prospect feels the need to make a decision.

Conceived more than fifty years ago, The Sandler Sales Methodology is among the oldest out there and still in popular use. In this methodology, rep's become advisors and build mutual trust with the customer through the qualification process driven with pain questions. The three core elements of Sandler are lead qualification, rapport building, and deal closing. Organizations that favor this methodology appreciate the needs assessment that opens the door to opportunities or indicates to reps that they must cut bait and move on to other prospects with needs that match their offerings.

Solution Selling gained notoriety in the 1980s and is a highly prescriptive approach to presenting the benefits that a custom solution can provide the customer. It still works today in certain sales contexts because it is predicated on the informed buyer. By shaping how customer interaction occurs, salespeople focus on problem resolution based on their offerings and take control of the sale.

There are many sales methodologies not listed here. They may be just as good or better for your organization's sales context, but because I'm not personally familiar with them, I wasn't comfortable listing them.

Sales methodology selection should be based on the buyer persona and which methodology is best suited to the buying process of your target customer group. Ultimately the right methodology is the one that best demonstrates how the customer's needs can be addressed by your products or services.

Sales Methodology Implementation

Prior to the widespread availability of software applications to assist in training and coaching, I used rudimentary methods to implement sales skill development and sales methodologies.

Since the beginning of our sales organization, every person in sales and marketing went through Gustav Käser Training International, providing effective sales techniques for all that attended. Gustav Käser also offered leadership training to those of us in supervisory roles. For each cohort, there were several sessions purposely spread throughout the year to build upon the previous material and for retention purposes. To reinforce the training, during our weekly fifteen-minute call huddle, a rep would be designated to share in two minutes or less how a sales technique was applied and to highlight the takeaway for the rest of the team. In the field, sales leaders would have reps focus on themes for the month to hone specific sales skills until they became innate. Each sales team member had personal proof on the effectiveness of the sales techniques, instilling confidence during sales conversations.

With a solid sales training foundation and product expertise, we were looking for years to adopt a formal sales methodology that was best suited for our premium and relatively complex products given our industry. Our B2C target groups, application solutions, B2B buying behavior, and the scientific proof that was needed to back the sales methodology led me to The Challenger Sale. *The Challenger Sale* book had just been published, and I was intrigued with the approach. I found myself attending executive sessions and being part of seminars where only a handful of other sales leaders across industries were asking direct questions and learning from the book's authors. Nowadays, Challenger is an international phenomenon, where conference centers and auditoriums are sold out. Armed with what I thought was sufficient knowledge on my part, after getting tenuous buy-in from sales leaders, there was a need to get the entire sales team aboard. I was committed to implementing this sales methodology that could be supported by the sales and leadership skills we developed through Gustav Käser Training International.

Prior to our national sales meeting, every rep took an assessment indicating which sales profile they fell into, and a development plan was provided to their sales leader. Every rep was sent a copy of *The Challenger Sale* book and asked to read it before the sales meeting. During the meeting, we had an open session about the findings in the book, and to see if there was general agreement with the methodology. If there was consensus on adoption, actual implementation of the methodology was next, and the real work began.

I'd like to say that everything I did got everyone up to speed in short order, but the truth is I had difficulty in implementing the sales methodology correctly and consistently across the sales organization. Even a couple of sales leaders seemed to be in a state of perpetual confusion, while the methodology was nebulous at best for many reps. It also didn't help that marketing was disengaged from the methodology, though that changed when I took over that department.

Realizing the errors of my ways, a full-blown re-rollout was executed. We hired a team from CEB (Challenger Sale parent company at the time) to work with our marketing department and planned a themed training that we launched during our national sales meeting, which included gamification through the use of a computer simulator. Prior to the meeting, I recruited a rep who was having success using aspects of The Challenger Sale methodology to be in videos that would serve as training resources for our sales team. These were done using a production company we had retained for numerous product and application videos. We had several scenes that focused on common B2B deals and product application selling. Largely a group of visual and hands-on learners, it wasn't until the sales professionals could actually see the methodology in action using common scenarios before it finally clicked. The star rep of the videos was a hilarious Long Island New Yorker, and the outtakes were gut busting, leaving most of us in tears after the screening.

Every regional and national sales meeting we had would include sales methodology reinforcement, mainly to get new additions to the team up to speed and keep everyone else on their toes. We would break the teams up into groups, mixing veteran reps with newbies and assigning them studies and performing simulations where they used the methodology in front of peers. It was a competition where points were assigned based on criteria that aligned with proper use of the methodology and sales techniques. As salespeople became more proficient, there was consistency, quicker sales cycles, and larger more complex sales closing.

There is a saying in sales of premium products, "cry once!" It pertains to making that large initial investment upfront to prevent the time, expense, and frustration of replacement and repurchase of inferior goods down the road. Through my Challenger Sales methodology implementation experience, I learned it is better to be all-in with implementation and have a robust reinforcement plan that includes interdepartmental support. In hindsight, I had the passion, but not the expertise to drive methodology adoption. After course correcting and creating a bullet proof implementation plan backed with knowledgeable resources, version two of the methodology rollout was successful.

CHAPTER 15

Contests, Awards, and Accolades

Sales contests tap into the competitive spirit of sales professionals and encourage desired behavior [xxvii]. Sales professionals get engaged and enjoy working toward contest results, when done right. Running sales contests the right way requires adherence to the following principles: align business objectives and metrics, track progress publicly, get teams involved, and offer incentives that are appealing to participants.

Aligning business objectives and metrics gets sales contests off to a good start. To garner support across functions, contests that drive desired behavior in tandem with strategy is more widely acceptable than a siloed approach that addresses a specific component of the sales process that may be disassociated with company objectives. Though even with aligned business objectives, using the wrong metrics will deflate the motivation of participants. Metrics that tell a different story than what they should be tracking or that create unfair advantages and subjective interpretations, will sink the contest before it gains steam. Metrics must be objective in accordance with goals and protected from manipulation.

Transparency of contest progress among participants, can be publicly displayed internally with the posting of metrics on a leaderboard. Accuracy and frequent updates to the data on the leaderboard lends credence to the contest through reliable tracking of performance. Leaving little wiggle room for dispute, transparent and accurate leaderboard contest data keeps sales professionals motivated for ongoing contest participation.

Contests designed around sales individuals are good, contests involving teams are better, and contests created for both are best. Teamwork should be rewarded, and the peer component adds additional motivation for sales professionals to strive for better results. What happens when a team dominates? That has a demoralizing effect on other teams that cannot compete and therefore lose motivation to continue to push competitively. Introducing incentives for individual contributions gives opportunities for individuals on different teams to shine in the limelight and be rewarded for their efforts. Separate individual leaderboards should also provide transparent tracking of individuals in the contest, so everyone knows where they stand and how much they are contributing.

Choose incentives wisely. Originality and tailoring of the carrot being dangled maintains focus on the prize. The incentive must be something that is appealing for everyone. Cash is always welcome, but for an office comprised of hardcore college football fans, opening day tickets shared among the winners will have much greater value. It isn't what the company wants to give, it is what the salespeople desire based on what the company is willing to budget for the prize.

With the principles of doing a sales contest fresh on our mind, we need to acknowledge there are elements of doing a contest wrong. Let's call those out and recognize them before they taint the contest.

The contest should be simple enough that a 10-year-old can understand it. Overcomplicating contests distracts focus on performance. Running multiple contests simultaneously is confusing for participants and also distracting. The same contests can have incentives for teams and individuals, but when additional and conflicting incentives are introduced that contradict the objectives of the other contests, it becomes a waste of effort and money, and makes leadership look foolish.

In addition to being simple, be inclusive. Contests designed around the top 10 percent of performers will exclude 90 percent of your team from engagement. Design contests that give everyone a fighting chance to elevate the performance of the sales organization and produce better outcomes.

Acknowledgments

Sales professionals not only want acknowledgements, they need acknowledgments. Sure, winning a sales contest is an acknowledgment. But that's not enough.

I encouraged the use of quarterly newsletters for the company to keep employees across departments informed of how we were all contributing to the business objectives, and also as a platform to acknowledge exceptional effort among sales professionals in the organization. Sales leaders would provide content about their teams, and I would edit the content into a succinct format for publication. Reps and their sales leaders would compete for the best acknowledgments in an ongoing contest between each other to showcase their achievements in front of the company.

Each year we would have annual awards for our salespeople. For example, per capita sales award, most new business, or greatest YoY growth awards. Winners would be announced at a company dinner during the days of our national sales meeting, where coworkers could celebrate their achievements together. The awards inspired reps, until our metric changed and the whole thing backfired.

The short of it was we changed the way we measured performance for a few awards where arguably the wrong reps/territories received the prizes. Aside from grumblings among the sales team, we faced more consequential effects. A rep with a territory that was undergoing an economic explosion and won a coveted award was let go a year later because his B2B dealers complained about his absence among other unprofessional things he'd been doing. The rookie that won the growth award ended up violating an HR policy with dire consequences, and by law we had to let him go. Finally, a consecutive-award-winning rep promoted to another sales role was struggling to keep his head above water a year later. When the awards ceremony rolled around and the first rep was announced, the rep was reluctant to stand up to receive the award. With mixed emotions, colleagues encouraged him to go to center stage, where I presented him with his award and the mic to say a few words. All he said was, "It's been nice working with you all!" Some reps laughed, some applauded, as the rest of us sales leaders turned beet red out of embarrassment. Needless to say, the awards ceremony went on hiatus for a year.

Along those lines I blew it with email accolades. The body of these emails were personalized, sincere, called out specific activities and results of the salesperson being honored among the sales team. My mistake was I started to put the salesperson's name receiving the accolade into the subject line instead of the accomplishment. That is until a trusting national sales manager called to my attention that reps were complaining about it because in the years past when someone's name was in the subject line of an email regardless of department, it meant their termination announcement. I still remember his exact words, "They came to me because I've told reps for years, if you see your name in the subject line of an email, don't bother to open it, just pack your bags." That was a bonehead move on my part, but at least I logged one more entry into my lessons learned file!

CHAPTER 16

Blind Spots

Companies have blind spots. That's a huge concern for employees, regardless of function. For SMB companies, the sales department is very often an afterthought. While sales professionals consider sales fundamentals to be given by default, companies have no concept of sales fundamentals, from sales structure to strategy, to basic sales skill development. They don't know what they don't know.

Brilliant and ambitious entrepreneurs start companies missing an appreciation for the critical role sales plays in their organization. A critical event presents a moment of clarity, where the Founders realize they need expertise, and they make the investment in hiring sales professionals (and other functions) imperative to the success of the organization. There's a lot going on as a business owner, and it's difficult to relinquish control, but sound businesspeople recognize their limitations and realize they need to bring in experts to address the company's blind spots.

Many companies bridge their need for expertise and budget limitations through professional service outsourcing. They pay only for services actually provided, greatly reducing overhead costs while having access to qualified resources. Legal outsourcing at times lasts through to the Enterprise level. Accounting is outsourced and heavily relied upon to keep the lights on. Marketing firms are hired to develop collateral and provide a marketing strategy. IT management firms are called in to handle all things computer-related or are used in part for data storage including Enterprise companies. Growing in popularity is outsourcing sales leadership.

Sales leadership consultants provide advantages that may not be realized with direct full-time hires. Unlike the possible trap of making bad employee hires, sales leadership consultants are hired on a contract basis that contains exit clauses to mitigate the risks for the business and the consultants.

Just as a business doesn't want to hire a consultant that is full of hot air, consultants don't want to work with businesses that are inflexible and unwilling to implement the change required. For the business it also means the comp package excludes costly health and fringe benefits offered to full-time employees, stock options, and other perks for the executive level hire. Instead of taking the risk of hiring a VP of Sales, they hire an outsourced Head of Sales and test the waters.

Sales management consultants follow frameworks that transcend their services, from diagnostics to implementation plans. They just change some specifics for each client. They follow a repeatable process that allows them to have multiple clients at once to earn more money and focus on varying aspects of the sales organization's needs with those different clients. For those select few owner-operators like me, everything we do is highly customized, and for more comprehensive projects, we only take one client at a time, ensuring our responsibilities have been fulfilled and the firm is well on its way to sales organizational success before we move on to the next firm. Either way, companies outsource their sales management to consultants in order to address blind spots, recognized and unrecognized.

Sales management consultants are baffled at first with what they discover during the diagnostic phase at their client's businesses. An overwhelming amount of work is required to put the basics in place and get them to a point where they can be managed by the firm. Those of us who have strong business acumen and have run organizations provide a holistic view, so we can make recommendations on how they impact other parts of the company more broadly.

Based on my own experience and of those outsourced sales management consultants I've come across, clients have the following most common blind spots:

- Sales goals (nonexistent)
- No sales strategy (TAM, lead gen, value prop)
- CRM partially used or not in place
- Tech stack (nonexistent)
- Sales process is haphazard
- Compensation incentive plans (nonexistent or ineffective)
- Sales hiring (unstructured and non EEOC compliant)
- Sales onboarding (limited or nonexistent)
- Sales skills and sales methodology (nonprescribed)
- Defunct sales leadership

Those are just the missing fundamentals. I have yet to come across an organization with world class team building for example, which compared to the above list of missing essentials, falls low on the priority list. For the fraction of businesses that hire sales professionals to shape their sales organization, the road to sales success is a long one but they are in a much better place than the majority of businesses that are unwilling to make the investment.

Even the best sales organization cannot succeed without effective interdepartmental collaboration. Leadership across functions must make a concerted effort to break down silos and get employees to work together to achieve the company's mission. From the company values to strategic intent, each departments' efforts must dovetail for strategic advantage and market success. An effective sales organization is the cornerstone of business, surrounded by the remaining departments to form an impenetrable structure.

There was a local small business I took on as a first client in my consulting venture. The company Founder, Rick, was in his golden years, a capricious inventor whose genius was offset only by his explosive temper. He was at the business every day and on weekends, continuously overseeing the lean and hardworking staff perhaps too closely when he wasn't working on inventions.

They were doing a lot of things right. I was impressed with their supply chain, about 90 percent of components sourced within 100 miles. They had the right amount of profitability baked into their products and had a handle on inventory—that is when Rick wasn't robbing parts for use on his projects without mentioning it to the general manager or anyone else. They had a niche product that was made in the USA, and they had been around for decades. The patents that protected the innovations on their flagship products had expired years ago, and knockoff companies had surpassed their sales. While they had sales through distribution, and offered repair service directly, they had reached their sales plateau.

It became obvious that the fundamentals of effective sales organization were nonexistent. I got to work right away, designing the sales org from scratch. In addition to putting out fires, I was drawing up sales force design for the company from soup to nuts. It was exciting and daunting at the same time. Remote distributor outreach was among the first items on the agenda. Then I got involved on the marketing side. I had a website redesign put into place, scheduled video content sessions with a local production company familiar with our products, and coordinated marketing collateral for publications in order to increase sales momentum.

Before long I found myself working the biggest tradeshow of the year for the industry. We had a relatively large booth, and our exhibition team was largely comprised of production and repair techs since it was too soon to have made a sales hire. Doing my backwards math in preparation for shows, I'd come up with sales goals for the costly, four-day show. I ran them across the company founder to ensure we would be able to deliver on units sold when we hit those numbers. He was excited because they had never rolled out a sales incentive plan like that before and because I had identified the profitability of the products being sold. I designed a tiered sales incentive plan that was lucrative for those working our booth and for the company.

The staff was reluctant to sell, though—they all said they weren't salespeople. I gave them some pointers, asked them to listen carefully before speaking and just have a conversation with customers, with the aim to keep everything positive all the time. When they were informed of the incentive plan, they suddenly became motivated to sell. Long story short, we exceeded the top tier goal, and the company had its best month of sales ever.

It really didn't take much to put them on a positive trajectory. Their story is very similar to many others. Company founders tend to be inventors, engineers, or generalist entrepreneurs. They usually have great products or services. They vet for solid staff. The company is generally operationally sound. Overall, these are nice businesses, or else they probably would not have survived.

Seldom do I come across any founders who have a sales background, and that's a huge blind spot. There have even been a couple that had recognized names as mentors in the sales field, yet sales remained a mystery. There is nuance and it takes time, but to me, putting sales fundamentals into place is not rocket science. Businesses that find themselves at sales plateaus just don't know what they don't know. This book will be a great help with demystifying sales, and identifying a sales professional for hire who can put sales fundamentals into place to unlock their company's full potential.

Conclusion

It's time to return to the cardinal rule of sales: no BS.

In the introduction to this book I pronounced that I wrote it for you, the sales rep, the sales leader, or the business professional working across functions with salespeople. At the time I truly believed that. It actually didn't dawn on me until these final chapters that the true intent was to write this book for my past self.

I wrote this book for that full commission rep who hadn't a clue, just motivation to survive and learn from unlikely mentors Bob and Tom. I wrote it for that sales rep who turned sales manager, who had to figure out how to lead on his own while pioneering a new brand. I wrote it for that guy who needed a holistic understanding of the sales org, the critical levers to pull, and the nuance required to take any sales organization to the next level. In the end I wrote this book for me. I wish I had this book as I built my sales career. It could have spared me from painful lessons and embarrassment. It would have fast tracked my development, and opened up all sorts of opportunities—no doubt. This is a resource for those of you in different parts of your professional journeys to do the right things and avoid the pitfalls I suffered along the way.

When you embarked on this journey, there may have been blind spots that pertained to sales. For those in non-selling functions, I hope the book title lived up to its name. For sales professionals, my hope is that blind spots have been addressed and insights can be put into practice for personal growth and company achievement. I wish you much success and every good thing in life!

Acknowledgments

There are numerous people who have shaped my career and whose tutelage led in large part to the lessons contained within this book. For their discretion, they will remain unnamed, but they know who they are.

Some specific callouts are due for those who dedicated their time to reviewing and providing feedback to the manuscript to help shape it into a completed work. Erika Taylor, your experience drawing upon twenty years working at The Walt Disney Company gave me confidence and provided corporate perspective to make necessary changes I would have missed. James Dunbar, your brutally honest and creative input set a path with my draft edits as you were the first to review the manuscript in its rawist form. Jon Thompson, as a trusted former coworker with sensitivity towards sales leadership, your input was invaluable. The thoroughness and thoughtfulness from Kiki Chryssogelos was much appreciated early on. Your professional background in sales at IBM, as well as your candor, came through with your suggestions. Speaking of candor, given the decades of experience at the senior level with enterprise companies, I took to heart the review Andrew Chryssogelos provided. Kiran Kaur, your experience as a journalist as well as in hiring talent for technology companies was a great contribution to the sales hiring chapter. For Greg Brown, my editor at Yellow Barn Creative, it was great to be in alignment throughout the editing passes. Your expertise refined and polished this work into something to be proud of.

Finally, the person I appreciate the most, Christina. As I stumbled into my sales career, you were by my side as my girlfriend and supported me as a traveling salesman as my wife. The additional burden of raising our older children nearly all on your own will never be forgotten. You always respected the commitment I had to my coworkers and understood how deep those relationships ran, even when they were at the expense of family time. You were supportive when I was considering embarking on this writing journey. Your help with the book's visuals exemplifies your willingness to support and be part of my endeavors. After all these years of struggle and sacrifice, you are still by my side, willing and able to take on the next challenge together. Words can't express how deeply I appreciate you.

Appendix I – Sales Titles

Account Executive (SMB/Enterprise) – Referred to as an AE, this is a front-line salesperson role who is responsible from sales pipeline stage III (discovery) on. The main focus is to secure new customers (*hunter*)/new logos, though growing existing business can be part of this role. AEs with SMB titles are focused on bringing in new small and mid-sized business. With smaller-sized clients, the sales process is accelerated since fewer decision makers are involved and there is less bureaucracy. AEs with Enterprise in their titles focus on large businesses with more than 1,000 employees and more than $1 billion in annual revenue. In part due to more opportunities, Enterprise AEs are tasked with growing existing business through cross selling (*farming*) as well as hunting for new business/new logos. Working with bigger organizations with more management layers and decision makers involved, the sales cycle is longer. Enterprise AEs are polished, prescriptive and comfortable selling into the C-suite.

Account Manager – Referred to as an AM, this is a *ranching* role where reps are tasked less with bringing in new clients and more with growing existing business. AMs are relationship builders.

Account Representative – Referred to as an AR, serves as the primary contact between clients and their company. ARs maintain existing customer accounts while also working to create new accounts in order to grow their territory.

Business Development Manager – Referred to as a BDM, responsibilities include building new key customer relationships; closing new business deals to improve the organizations market position; working with internal sales teams, marketing departments, and other managers to increase sales with new accounts.

Business Development Representative – Referred to as a BDR, this front-of-pipeline position is tasked with deep diving into qualifying new customers through research and cold outreach to *produce sales qualified leads* (SQRs).

Chief Sales Officer – An executive position where leadership, strategy, business development, and corporate branding to increase revenue and gross profit are the primary responsibilities. Similar to an Executive Vice President, the Large Enterprise CSO may have direct reports in charge of sales teams from different countries, product lines, or brands under the parent umbrella.

Customer Care Representative – Also known as CCRs and Customer Service Reps (CSRs), they are typically call center-based reps who handle customer complaints, process transactional sales orders, and provide information about the company's products and services.

Director of Sales – In an SMB, this role is a front-line sales management position that oversees the sales performance of regional sales reps. In Enterprise businesses, there may be one more reporting layer between front line sales reps and the DOS, possibly a regional sales manager or a district sales manager depending on the size of the sales force. The DOS executes on marching orders from the VP of Sales.

District Sales Manager – Manages sales teams within a specified geographic area and is responsible for helping direct reports execute on the sales plan.

Enterprise Sales Representative – Referred to as an ESR, the focus is on large businesses with more than 1,000 employees and more than $1 billion in annual revenue. ESRs are tasked with growing existing business through cross selling (farming) as well as hunting for new business. ESRs own the pipeline from Stage III (discovery) on. Working with bigger organizations with more management layers and decision makers involved, there is a long sales cycle. Enterprise AEs are polished, prescriptive and comfortable selling into the C-suite.

Head of Sales – Also known interchangeably as the VP of Sales, as part of the senior management team, strategic planning, sales force leadership, business process optimization and introduction of new technologies to assist the sales department are core responsibilities. Ultimately, the responsibility of meeting sales revenue, profitability, and budgetary objectives rest on this role.

Inside Sales Representative – This is a catchall title for sales roles strictly inside an office or call center, where prospective customers are not visited in person. Instead, phone, email, and web conferencing are used. In a stricter sense, inside sales reps are assigned accounts that fall into a tertiary sales quadrant where the ROI for outside sales reps is net negative, and therefore it takes some of the work burden off outside sales reps to keep them focused on customers with greater revenue potential. The general consensus is that inside sales is growing at a significantly larger rate faster than outside sales, those surveyed indicate approximately a 15 percent increase. Included into this bucket are SDRs, CCRs/CSRs, and BDRs among others. Inside sales representatives are also being referred to as *remote* because there's an increasing trend to have these sales professionals work from home and across the globe rather than a central office or location.

Inside Sales Manager – The ISM is usually a front-line manager tasked with managing inside sales teams to ensure revenue objectives are met.

Jobber – This niche specific sales role is B2C, where the jobber goes direct to the customer's business and sells products out of a truck or van, the sale is transactional. An exemplar jobber, Mac Tool reps that have designated territories with established routines to visit automotive shops that may be in need of hand tools in a pinch or because they are usually overwhelmed to go to a tool house.

Key Account Manager – The KAM builds and nurtures what are considered to be high-value customers. Predicated on the 80/20 rule, a salesperson (KAM) dedicated to the top 20 percent of accounts that bring in 80 percent of the business, the Kam helps retains some of the company's best customers by being a dedicated resource to help these customers realize their business goals.

Market Development Manager – This is typically a front-line sales rep role with a market research component. Being in the field, the MDM builds relationships between multiple accounts and acts as a source of market trend intelligence.

Marketing Manager – This role is a front-line sales rep position with a marketing component. Tasked with growing the territory with new and existing customers, the MM also coordinates with the company's marketing department to leverage advertising collateral on behalf of customers.

National Accounts Manager – The NAM is point person on managing accounts that are found across the country and impact different regions. Due to their magnitude, these accounts may have greater buying power and influence which can impact SMB businesses in different regions across the nation. The NSM is tasked with mitigating disruption between national accounts and SMB accounts, while growing/expanding national accounts.

National Sales Manager – In smaller businesses, the NSM fills the responsibilities described previously of the NAM. In larger companies, the NSM leads direct reports such as KAMs, and Regional Sales Managers to grow over all sales in a collaborative manner.

Outside Sales Representative – These windshield warriors are expected to be face-to-face with customers in the field daily. They provide hands-on explanations of new and existing products, train customers sales staff on how to sell products from their brand, take inventory for customers, and generally attend to the customers business needs. In this bucket fall all front-line sales reps that make in person sales calls such as AMs, ARs, BDMs, ESRs, KAMs, and MMs among others. Field sales roles and the cost to fund them are expensive for companies requiring that the revenue potential is high to justify the requisite costs.

Regional Sales Manager – An RSM in a SMB may have similar responsibilities as an AR, but with a massive territory. In large companies, the RSM oversees sales reps within the region, coaches/develops the regional sales team to hit goals, and takes a hands-on role to move sales forward with direct reports in the region. The RSM reports into a sales director and VP of Sales.

Sales Associate – This title is commonly used to described sales staff in retail stores. They greet customers, answer questions, and help customers with refunds and returns.

Strategic Accounts Manager – SAMs are another layer to the key account manager focus, zeroing in on specific large key accounts within a region (e.g. Home Depot in the Southeastern US). SAMs are individual contributors.

Sales Engineer – The role of an SE is to sell complex and highly technical products or services to businesses. In larger organizations with offering that command a high price, are complicated, and may require integration, an SE may be partnered with an AE to close the sale and ensure the customer's expectations are met or exceeded.

Sales Jockey – Slang term used to describe typical outside salespersons, usually those who travel long distances between accounts and that own the entire sales pipeline. Also known as road warriors.

Sales Operations – Title preceded with VP of, Director of, or referred to as sales operations manager, depending on the size and complexity of the business. Sales ops commonly reports into the VP of Sales. This is an administrative position that has become increasingly more popular and important. Grounded in data analysis and process, this role is tasked with sales force optimization. Areas of focus include tech stack selection, performance metrics analysis, growth forecasting, and overall sales process optimization.

Sales Representative – Catchall name used to refer to salespeople that promote a particular brand of product or service.

Territory Sales Manager – TSM is another title used interchangeably with regional sales manager though the RSM title is more common. Roles and responsibilities are the same as RSMs.

VP of Sales (EVP) – Also known interchangeably as the Head of Sales, as part of the senior management team, strategic planning, sales force leadership, business process optimization and introduction of new technologies to assist the sales department are core responsibilities. Ultimately, the responsibility of meeting sales revenue, profitability, and budgetary objectives rest on this role. At the Enterprise level, there may be an Executive VP of Sales with these responsibilities that has VP of Sales from different countries, product lines, or brands under the parent umbrella, report into them.

VP of Sales Operations – The VPSO is on the hook for the overall effectiveness and productivity of the sales organization including inside and outside sales. Focused on optimizing process, the VPSO works cross functionally within the organization and typically reports to the EVP. As tech stacks become more robust and inside sales functions outpace outside sales, the need for VSOPs is growing.

Glossary

Activity Dominator – a salesperson who thrives in an activity-rich environment.

Active reference – a referral source who acts as a personal ambassador of another person.

Ambivert – a blend of personality traits that falls between the introvert-extrovert continuum.

Anchoring – using the power of suggestion, price anchoring establishes a jump off point in negotiation.

Application Tracking System (ATS) – sorting software that assists companies for hiring and recruitment.

Best Alternative to a Negotiated Agreement (BATNA) – the best outside option should negotiations reach an impasse. Identifying a negotiator's BATNA informs negotiation strategy.

Behavioral Contagion – the propensity to copy the behavior of others within vicinity. It pertains to following other people to an assembled crowd or making a purchase after seeing someone else buy.

Business to Business (B2B) – business-to-business commercial transactions.

Business to Consumer (B2C) – when businesses sell directly to consumers.

Clawbacks – a contractual provision where money or benefits that have been given are required to be returned due to special circumstances.

Closed ended questions – questions that can be answered with "yes" or "no."

Closing – a term likely borrowed from a real estate in reference to the final step in the transaction; it means making a sale.

Coachability – the ability to listen, absorb, and execute on advice given by coworkers to become better at a role.

Cold Calling – when sales reps reach out to unknown prospective customers who have not expressed interests in the products or services of the rep.

Compensation Management Software (CMS) – allows organizations to plan and execute on compensation.

Contact (pipeline) – the first stage in the sales pipeline, also referred to where prospecting and lead generation are incorporated with outreach to facilitate interest.

Contact Center as a Service (CCaas) – contact center software hosted in the cloud.

Cross selling – selling an additional product or service to an existing customer, such as an accessory for a product being purchased.

Customer Lifetime Value (CLV) – a formula that predicts the profit attributed to the future relationship of a customer.

Customer Relationship Management (CRM) – technology for managing customer relationships, interactions, and prospecting for new customers.

Dashboard – a succinct graphic interface that conveys key performance indicators for the user.

Dials – number of phone calls.

Discovery – gathering information about the customer's unique needs, interests, and motivation to help inform the buying process.

Early adopters – individuals or organizations who use a new innovation, product, or technology well before others.

Early majority – a large group of the population who tries new products after early adopters and innovators.

Emotional Intelligence (EQ) – Emotional Quotient, the capacity to control emotions, handling interpersonal relationships in a smart, objective manner to encourage growth and support.

Enterprise - large businesses with more than 1,000 employees and more than $1 billion in annual revenue.

Equal Employment Opportunity Commission (EEOC) – federal agency charged with enforcing laws regarding discrimination and harassment among employees and job applicants in the United States.

Extrovert – a type of person who is energized by being around other people; typically, gregarious and unreserved.

Fair Labor Standards Act – federal law that set standards for minimum wage, overtime pay, record keeping, and child labor in the United States.

Farming – getting more business out of existing clients, nurturing existent client relationships.

Firefighting – a term referring to crisis management in the sales function, typically among sales managers.

Gross Market Value (GMV) – a key metric used among marketplaces that calculates all the goods or services sold in the marketplace over a given period of time.

Haircut – slang term referring to undervaluing ones pay.

Hero kit – essential repair parts for on-the-spot basic service needs to help customers out in the field.

Hot Leads – customers who show interest in buying a product or service through buying signals.

Human Resources (HR) – organizational function that deals with issues related to people such as compensation, hiring, onboarding, performance management, terminations, and organizational development.

Hunting – a sales role that chases new leads and new sales.

Inbound leads – potential customers drawn in through brand information, insights, and incentives.

Innovation adoption curve – classification of users into categories based on their appetite to adopt new technology.

Innovators – the least numerous group in the diffusion of innovations theory, they are the earliest to adopt new technology.

Inside sales – sales representatives who work inside an office and do not visit customers in person.

Introvert – a reserved and reflective personality that enjoys time spent alone more than time spent with groups.

Key Performance Indicator (KPI) – a performance measurement that evaluates the success of a particular objective or activity for an organization.

Kicker – designed to incentivize reps to overachieve quota; additional financial rewards are provided for over target earnings.

Laggards – traditionalists and the last group of hold outs to adopt new technologies, usually because they have no choice due to obsolescence of previous-generation technologies.

Late majority – large segment of population who is willing to adopt a new technology only after seeing it adopted by the majority of the population and becoming ubiquitous.

Latency – delay in response or time to respond to a lead.

Lead scoring – a method of ranking prospective customers based on the value each lead represents for the company.

Leaderboard – a visual ranking of names and positions of competitors among sales professionals.

Leads – prospective customers.

Learning Management Systems (LMS) – software applications designed for training, development, and learning programs.

Line card – a representative list in a brochure of brands, products, and services sold by a third party.

Marketing Qualified Leads (MQL) – prospective customer brought in through marketing efforts.

Marketplace – an online entity that connects buyers and sellers.

Master distributors – a wholesale distributor that sells products through other distributors.

Meaningful conversations – conversations with target customer persona's that fall within time parameters and tick sales-trigger boxes.

Mirroring – a rapport building technique where the rep adopts the verbal and physical behaviors of the customer.

New logos – also known as new brands, referring to new business acquisition for hunting activities at the corporate or enterprise level.

Open ended questions – questions that begin with how, what, when where, and why, they must be answered in the respondent's own words and cannot be answered with a "yes" or "no" answer.

Outbound leads – direct emails or phone calls where the rep reaches out initially to the prospect.

Outside sales – sales reps who meet customers in person or visit work sites to sell products or services. Also known as field sales.

On Target Earnings (OTE) – the variable portion of pay when a sales professional hits quota goal.

Product line – a single brand of products sold by the same company.

Proposal – a document where the rep outlines the scope of products or services to buyers for purchase.

Purchase Order (PO) – an official commitment by the buyer to pay the seller for specific products or services to be delivered in the future.

Qual call – a qualification stage usually involving a phone call where discovery questions are used and leads are determined on level of interest.

Qualification – determining customer intent in the buying process.

Ragnar – overnight running relays, created and organized by Ragnar Events, LLC.

Ranching – a sales role that balances hunting and farming activities.

Reciprocity – an equal benefit in a relationship when there is an even exchange.

Regression analysis – a statistical procedure for determining a relationship between a dependent variable and independent variables for a given population, expressed as an equation for a line or a curve.

Request for Proposal (RFP) – bid documents that outline specifications and offerings of required products and services.

Retention – engaging existing customer to keep them buying the company's products and remaining loyal to the brand.

Return on Sales (ROS) – used to evaluate a company's operational efficiency, it is determined by dividing operating profit by net sales.

Robo Dialers – also known as auto dialers; software that automatically dials phone numbers and connects recipients to recordings or live operators.

Sales Asset Management (SAM) – software designed to help organizations manage marketing collateral, internal reference material, and all other sales assets in a central repository.

Sales Development Rep (SDR) – an inside sales position typically tasked with lead generation and the early stage of the sales pipeline.

Sales Enablement – a process designed around the buyer to help salespeople be more effective through relevant tools, content, and information.

Sales Engagement Platform (SEP) – technology that provides a means to provide content to customers, monitors customer engagement, offers sophisticated analytics for sales optimization, and identifies skill gaps for sales training.

Sales funnel – also known as the purchase funnel, revenue funnel, or sales process, refers to steps in the buying process that companies lead customers through.

Sales methodology – guiding principles to help salespeople successfully navigate steps within the sales process.

Sales motion – the specific sales method a company uses to deliver a product or service to the customer.

Sales pipeline – organized customer flow through clearly defined sales stages that help sales professionals stay organized, recognize sales triggers, and be more efficient in their role.

Sales pitch – in the strictest sense, a canned presentation given to prospective customers. It generally refers to a salesperson's attempt to sell a customer on a product or service.

Sales playbook – an information resource containing sales scripts, answers to sales objections, and tactical plays addressing scenarios encountered in the buying environment.

Sales Productivity – revenue generated by the sales organization through efficiency and effectiveness of the sales force.

Sales Qualified Leads (SQL) – a prospective customer who has been researched and vetted by members of the sales team.

Sales Readiness – certification of necessary skills and knowledge required for salespeople to have effective communication with buyers.

Search Engine Marketing (SEM) – internet marketing utilizing paid search advertising to increase search engine page rankings for better customer visibility.

Search Engine Optimization (SEO) – method of organically increasing quality and quantity of traffic to websites.

Sell up – to advocate for oneself to a superior or boss, highlight accomplishments, or make persons of higher organizational position aware of one's contributions.

Small to Midsize Businesses (SMB) – organizations with less than 100 employees and that generate less than $50 million in annual revenue are considered small businesses. Midsize businesses have fewer than 1,000 employees, but more than 100 employees, and generate more than $50 million in revenue annually.

Software as a Service (SaaS) – coinciding with the rise of cloud-based computing, SaaS is software accessed through an external server and charged to customers as a subscription.

Spreadsheet management – a derogatory term for making bad strategic decisions based solely on the numbers in a spreadsheet without taking into consideration market conditions and human factors.

Systems – technology typically used to support an organization's internal network for more efficient business operation.

Tag lines – marketing term referring to a catchphrase or a slogan.

Triad – a tribal leadership relationship where a third person bonds and mentors the other two.

Upselling the act of leveling up the purchase of a product to a customer who may have initially wanted a less expensive product or service.

Upside – sales vernacular for a financially upward trend.

Voice over Internet Protocol (VoIP) – technology that allows voice to be transmitted over the internet or digital network rather than traditional phone lines.

Warm leads – a prospective customer that has shown signs of interest for a company's product or service.

Win rate – percentage of sales opportunities proposed/quoted and won.

Year over Year (YoY) – a method of evaluating measured events on an annual basis.

Yellow Pages – a hard-copy telephone directory printed on thin yellow paper.

References

[i] https://hbr.org/2011/01/the-dirty-secret-of-effective

[ii] https://www.forbes.com/sites/amymorin/2014/11/23/7-scientifically-proven-benefits-of-gratitude-that-will-motivate-you-to-give-thanks-year-round/#3801b9ea183c

[iii] Duckworth, Angela. *Grit: The Power of Passion and Perseverance.* New York, NY, Scribner. 2006.

[iv] https://www.mimesysvr.com/

[v] *American Pickers.* History. 2010-20.

[vi] Grant, Adam M. "Rethinking the Extraverted Sales Ideal: The Ambivert Advantage," *Psychological Science.* June 2013.

[vii] *2011 MLC Customer Purchase Research Survey.* Marketing Leadership Council. CEB. 2011.

[viii] http://customerthink.com/neuroscience-confirms-we-buy-on-emotion-justify-with-logic-yet-we-sell-to-mr-rational-ignore-mr-intuitive/

[ix] Rogers, Everett M. *Diffusion of Innovations, 5th edition.* New York, NY, Free Press. 2013.

[x] https://hbr.org/2006/07/ending-the-war-between-sales-and-marketing

[xi] Allen, Terina. "How Bad Bosses Compel Good Employees To Leave." *Forbes,* Forbes Magazine, 21 Sept. 2019, www.forbes.com/sites/terinaallen/2019/09/21/how-bad-bosses-compel-good-employees-to-leave/.

[xii] Houston, Elaine. "The Importance of Emotional Intelligence (Including EI Quotes)." *PositivePsychology.com,* 18 Feb. 2020, positivepsychology.com/importance-of-emotional-intelligence/.

[xiii] Goleman, Daniel (2012). Emotional Intelligence; Why it can Matter More than IQ. New York, NY, Bantam Books.

[xiv] Megías-Robles A, Gutiérrez-Cobo MJ, Gómez-Leal R, Cabello R, Gross JJ, Fernández-Berrocal P (2019) Emotionally intelligent people reappraise rather than suppress their emotions. PLoS ONE 14(8): e0220688. https://doi.org/10.1371/journal.pone.0220688

[xv] Stein, Steven, and Howard E. Book. *The EQ Edge: Emotional Intelligence and Your Success*. John Wiley, 2006.

[xvi] Bradberry, Travis, Greaves, Jean. (2009). Emotional Intelligence 2.0. San Diego, CA, TalentSmart.

[xvii]   Zettelmeyer, Florian. "A Leader's Guide to Data Analytics." *Kellogg Insight*, 2015, insight.kellogg.northwestern.edu/article/a-leaders-guide-to-data-analytics.

[xviii] Allport, Gordan W. and Postman, Leo (1947). *The Psychology of Rumor*, New York, NY, Henry Holt and Company

[xix] https://news.gallup.com/businessjournal/162953/tackle-employees-stagnating-engagement.aspx

[xx] https://employeeengagement.com/wp-content/uploads/2013/04/2012-Q12-Meta-Analysis-Research-Paper.pdf

[xxi] https://www.forbes.com/sites/brianscudamore/2016/03/09/why-team-building-is-the-most-important-invest ment-youll-make/#710bf566617f

[xxii] https://www.gallup.com/workplace/269405/high-performance-workplaces-differently.aspx?utm_source=workplace-newsletter&utm_medium=email&utm_campaign=WorkplaceNewsletter_Jan_012 12020&utm_content=Type-TextLink-1&elqTrackId=27f16148f02c420496cc1cbe8e09a166&elq=b806f5bb34574455a32 acfd7644c5612&elqaid=3132&elqat=1&elqCampaignId=696

[xxiii]   Logan, David, et al. *Tribal Leadership: Leveraging Natural Groups to Build a Thriving Organization*. Harper Paperbacks, 2011.

[xxiv] https://hbr.org/2015/09/the-7-attributes-of-the-most-effective-sales-leaders.

[xxv] https://www.jobvite.com/jobvite-news-and-reports/2019-recruiting-benchmark-report-your-guide-to-finding-top-talent/

[xxvi] Homburg, C., Wieseke, J. & Kuehnl, C. Social influence on salespeople's adoption of sales technology: a multilevel analysis. *J. of the Acad. Mark. Sci.* 38, 159–168 (2010). https://doi.org/10.1007/s11747-009-0157-x

[xxvii] Murphy, W.H., Dacin, P.A. & Ford, N.M. Sales contest effectiveness: An examination of sales contest design preferences of field sales forces. *JAMS* **32,** 127–143 (2004). https://doi.org/10.1177/0092070303261582

Index

O

Objections · 62
Office Day · 42, 43
On Target Earning · 259
Onboarding · 74, 89, 139, 164, 165, 166,
167, 193, 202, 221, 238, 257
Open Ended Question · 60, 259
Open House · 63
Outbound Leads · 259
Outside Sales · 14, 36, 39, 42, 126, 130,
140, 196, 250, 253, 259
Outside Sales Representative · 251
Over Target Earnings · 174, 257

P

Phonetic Alphabet · 68, 69
Pink, Daniel · ii
Pipeline · 2, 19-28, 31, 36, 44, 71, 77,
143, 193, 215, 255, 260, 261
Pitch · 25, 48, 65, 189, 261
Pitch Deck · 22
Planning · vi, 42, 44, 65, 102, 109, 110,
126, 129, 133, 135, 185
Playbook · 94, 196, 200, 261
Position Description · 140, 141, 142,
145, 164
Positivity · 55, 97
Predictive Index · 161, 162
President · 18, 90, 91, 92, 100
Pricing · 56-58, 78
Process · 197, 198, 199, 200
Product Line · iii, 10, 57, 259
Proposal · 25, 259
Purchase Order · 10, 208, 259

Q

Qual call · 23, 259
Qualification · 23, 25, 226, 259

R

Ragnar · 135, 259
Ranching · 259
Rebuttals · 62
Reciprocity · 72, 73, 259
Recruitment · 122, 151, 152
Regional Sales Manager · 252, 253
Regression Analysis · 198, 259
Request For Proposal · 260
Retention · 26, 27, 80, 81, 182, 195, 260
Return On Sales · 182, 260
RingCentral · 212
Robo Call · 213, 214
Robo Dialers · 213, 214, 215, 260

S

SaaS · 140, 262
Sales Asset Management · 220, 260
Sales Associate · 252
Sales Coaching · 110, 220
Sales Cycle · 23, 32, 113, 139, 180, 248
Sales Development Rep · 260
Sales Director · 252
Sales Engagement Platform · 220, 260
Sales Engineer · 252
Sales Jockey · 252
Sales Methodology · 149, 162,193, 224,
226, 230, 260
Sales Motion · 190, 260
Sales Operations · 252
Sales Productivity Tools · 221
Sales Qualified Leads · 261
Sales Readiness · 221, 261
Sales Representative · 253
Sandler Sales · 226
Scale · 203-204
Search Engine Marketing · 22, 261
Search Engine Optimization · 22, 261
Self-Motivation · 106
Selling Up · ii, 49, 209

Made in the USA
Middletown, DE
19 February 2021

33800742R00170